For the home baker with a sense of fun and a desire for creative new formulas, **BREAKING BAO** features 88 foolproof recipes for an inventive array of cakes, cookies, buns, mochi, mooncakes, donuts, and savory snacks. This collection is celebrated pastry chef Clarice Lam's love letter to both time-honored and modern baking techniques, as well as to the bold, textured, sweet, and savory flavors of Asia.

A daughter of parents from Hong Kong, Lam layers the nostalgic tastes of her childhood with the flavors of her travels and the methods she developed in the kitchens at The Chocolate Room, Kimika, Thomas Keller's Bouchon Bakery, and Jean-George Vongerichten's Spice Market.

- Her deep adolescent love of Totino's Pizza Rolls informs her Gochujang Pizza Rolls, which marry salami with gochujang and mozzarella.

- Her lime pie is a study in contrasts: a crust of salty and buttery Ritz, a creamy custard with a beguiling lick of pandan, and a cloud of meringue.

- Her earthy Matcha Shortbread gets a bittersweet edge from a frosting of Raspberry Ganache.

- Pork floss and scallions top Lam's big-flavor focaccia.

And the eponymous bao: Lam devotes a chapter to these toothsome baked, fried, and steamed buns. Her interpretations take various shapes—babka loaves, mochi, round rolls—and flavors, including sweet corn, kimchi, Bolognese, chocolate banana, and Vietnamese cinnamon.

A trove of unique confections and irresistible snacks, **BREAKING BAO** will fuel your creativity and fill your belly for years to come.

Br

eaking Bao

88 Bakes
and Snacks
from Asia
and Beyond

Clarice Lam

Photography by Evan Sung

CHRONICLE BOOKS
SAN FRANCISCO

Library of Congress Cataloging-in-Publication Data

Names: Lam, Clarice, author. | Sung, Evan, photographer.
Title: Breaking Bao : 88 bakes and snacks from Asia and
  beyond / Clarice Lam ; photography by Evan Sung.
Description: San Francisco : Chronicle Books, [2024] |
  Includes index.
Identifiers: LCCN 2024017856 | ISBN 9781797225234
  (hardback)
Subjects: LCSH: Baking. | Snacks. | Cakes. | Desserts. |
  LCGFT: Cookbooks.
Classification: LCC TX763 .L265 2024 | DDC 641.7/1--dc23/
  eng/20240503
LC record available at https://lccn.loc.gov/2024017856

Manufactured in Italy.

Prop and set styling by Guillermo Riveros.
Prop assistance by Audris Lam.
Food styling by Clarice Lam.
Design by Vanessa Dina.
Typesetting by Wynne Au-Yeung.

10 9 8 7 6 5 4 3 2 1

Chronicle books and gifts are available at special quantity discounts to corporations, professional associations, literacy programs, and other organizations. For details and discount information, please contact our premiums department at corporatesales@chroniclebooks.com or at 1-800-759-0190.

Chronicle Books LLC
680 Second Street
San Francisco, California 94107
www.chroniclebooks.com

To Mommy and Daddy,
for always telling me to eat.

BAO 33

CAKES & DESSERTS

SNACKS

Introduction

In my seventh-grade history class, each student was asked to bring in some sort of food or treat that represented their culture to share with the rest of the class. It was meant to be a lesson in the importance of learning about each other, giving out little pieces of your background for others to enjoy. Immediately, I knew what I'd bring: White Rabbit, my favorite candy from Hong Kong. White Rabbit is a delicious, creamy confection that resembles a white Tootsie Roll with a texture like that of a Starburst. Each cylinder of chewy-yet-toothsome sweet milk candy is wrapped in a thin sheet of rice paper with about a half inch of overhang that serves no purpose other than to instantly glue the entire candy to your inner lower lip. My sister and I would shake our heads side to side and see how long the candy could hang on before falling off our faces. These were candies that, even at such a young age, carried memories for me, candies that brought me a deep happiness that I was eager to share with my class, candies that held weight.

Unfortunately, nobody in my class shared my enthusiasm. Instead of having fun with the rice paper overhang like my sister and I did, my classmates tried peeling off all the rice paper. Even after I explained to them it was edible, they all just found it too "weird" even to taste. I returned to my desk heartbroken among a sea of uneaten White Rabbits. Back then, so many of the things I enjoyed with my family were "weird," so it's unsurprising that I eventually grew tired of explaining and defending my culture and succumbed to the pressure to fit in and be the best "American" I could be.

My parents met each other at university in Toronto, Canada, where I was born. My father, a jolly man with Buddha x Homer Simpson vibes, was born in a small village in China. His father, originally from the Philippines, would eventually return there, leaving the rest of the family to escape communist China on their own. My dad has 101 stories of navigating through the mountains as a child alongside his brother with my grandmother guiding them. Eventually, they made it onto a raft and floated to the safety of Hong Kong.

My mother, a nonstop giggler and snacker with major green M&M vibes, spent her childhood in British-ruled Hong Kong before moving to Toronto for high school. Her mother, hailing from Shanghai, had an affinity for all the finer things in life, especially French cheeses.

When I was five years old, we moved to Los Angeles, where my sister would be born. We grew up in a very non-diverse suburb, and we stuck out like a sore thumb. My schooling experience was terrible. I was constantly bullied and mocked for being and looking "different." When I was ten, my dad's job moved us to Hong Kong, where my parents enrolled me in the French International School. Being surrounded daily by the children of wealthy European and British businesspeople in Hong Kong did not do my self-esteem any favors. Once again, I found myself ridiculed and alienated in the country that I thought would accept me.

While these moves were tough on me emotionally, the silver lining was always the food. While based in Hong Kong, we traveled extensively throughout Asia, dining everywhere from local street markets to fancy restaurants adorned with golden chopstick holders.

After a few years, we moved back to Los Angeles. My parents continued to travel to far-off places, and each time they would return with a whole suitcase filled with local snacks. My sister and I thrived on the different flavored chips and confections they'd bring to us. It felt like Christmas morning each time I opened up a suitcase loaded with foreign treats just waiting for me to taste them.

A month after turning seventeen and graduating high school, I received a modeling contract in San Francisco and left home. This eventually led me on a fourteen-year-long tour of the world as a mediocre model and professional nomad. I had the privilege of finding myself time and time again in different corners of the world. Each country felt like a new beginning, but everywhere I went, one thing remained the same: I was constantly reminded that I didn't belong. Back then I was hard to miss, standing at 5 feet 10 inches and 110 pounds. People who had not grown up around many Asians treated me like I was on display at a traveling freak show.

It felt like no matter where I went, nobody could relate to me as a human. It seemed to me that, in everyone else's eyes, my entire identity revolved around my ethnic background. I didn't want to talk about how Asian or what Asian I was anymore, and it made me shy away from anything that would point back to my heritage, including the cuisine.

Each new home became another chance for me to try to fit in and find acceptance, and with that came studying the local cuisine and culture. While living in Europe and the United Kingdom for about a decade, I discovered the power of the dinner party to bridge cultural gaps through food and community. While living in Paris, I couldn't walk past a bakery without a huge smile on my face. I gazed at the walls laden with boules and baguettes and the display case filled with perfectly laminated croissants begging for me to pick them apart, layer by layer. It was then that I knew I would become a pastry chef.

Becoming a chef would be the perfect way not only to explore and appreciate different cuisines but to relearn how to appreciate my own. There is a plethora of foods that exist in different iterations all over the world and dishes that can be traced back through their many transformations. For example, flan—whether it's called a custard, steamed in a dish, or baked in a shell of pastry—exists universally. A Chinese scallion pancake makes it way south and turns into a roti canai in Malaysia, and then west to become a roti or chapati in India. Training to become a chef would allow me special access to these interwoven food histories that had given me solace when the rest of the world shut me out.

My journey became a testament to my resilience and self-discovery. I thought to myself, *if food is all connected, then people certainly must be, too.* I questioned how I could present myself and my experiences through food. I thought back on my seventh-grade history class and the White Rabbit candy as a symbol of my cultural identity and the challenges I faced each time I wanted to share anything. I realized that "weird" actually equates to "unfamiliar." When I became a chef, I considered how I could make the unfamiliar familiar and approachable. I wanted everyone to be able to enjoy all the things from around the globe that I enjoyed without hesitation or judgment, and in a way that would connect them to their own individual histories.

My book highlights my love for Asian flavors while simultaneously connecting the dots between cultures. It will give you a gateway to restaurant- and bakery-quality recipes that are accessible to make in any home kitchen. Beyond the baking, I will guide you through the world of popular Asian ingredients, making them approachable for unfamiliar palates while offering a fresh perspective for those already initiated.

Breaking Bao is a culinary journey bridging gaps between Asian flavors and global techniques. It is a collection of recipes rooted in my personal journey of self-discovery and the transformative power of embracing one's heritage. With humor, whimsy, and respect for traditions, I invite you to sit with me to break bread, barriers, and bao, all at the same table.

Ingredients

We've all heard the saying "you are what you eat." Similarly, your bake is only as good as its ingredients. Here I've highlighted some familiar and unfamiliar ingredients that make an appearance in this book, along with descriptions and brand suggestions to help you make the most of your baking experience.

Flours & Starches

Let's talk about different types of flours and why the protein content matters. In wheat flours there are two types of protein, glutenin and gliadin. These proteins are activated with the addition of a liquid such as water or milk. When mixed or kneaded, these best friends link up and form a strong bond, forming strands of gluten. If you witnessed the sourdough starter craze in recent years, you should remember that strong starters look like a bubbly network of cobwebs layered over one another. It's the same idea when it comes to gluten in baking. The higher the protein content, the stronger the network, which means the higher the capability of developing more gluten and supporting gases that are produced while fermenting and/or baking.

Whereas developing the gluten structure in food like bread is good, you would not want that same texture for a tender cake or chewy cookie. And that is why we use different flours for different applications.

ALL-PURPOSE FLOUR is also known as **WHITE FLOUR** or **PLAIN FLOUR** outside of the United States. It is the most widely used and versatile flour, milled from a combination of hard and soft wheat, typically at an 80:20 ratio, with approximately 12 percent protein. All-purpose flour is great for baking anything from cookies to pies, breakfast pastries, some cakes, and quick breads. I use King Arthur flour in all of my recipes.

BREAD FLOUR is a high-protein flour made solely from hard wheat, and generally contains 13 to 14 percent protein. Higher protein means the ability to develop more gluten, which yields more stretch, elasticity, and a nice chew in breads. Because of the structure provided by its protein content, using bread flour also helps baked goods rise and stay nice and tall. I use King Arthur bread flour.

BUCKWHEAT FLOUR is neither a grain nor a grass; it's considered a pseudocereal and shares this category with ingredients such as quinoa and amaranth. Buckwheat is super high in dietary fiber, amino acids, and protein, and despite "wheat" in the name, it contains no gluten. It is used widely in Europe and Asia and has a very distinctive flavor: earthy, savory, nutty, grassy; it's very black sesame-y on the nose. I use Bob's Red Mill buckwheat flour.

CAKE FLOUR has the lowest protein content of all the flours at around 7.5 to 9 percent. Made purely of soft wheat, this flour has a distinct fragrance like faint vanilla and is ideal for baking anything with a light and fluffy texture: cakes, delicate pastries, and tender biscuits. I use Swan's Down cake flour.

GLUTINOUS RICE FLOUR is also known as **STICKY RICE FLOUR** or **SWEET RICE FLOUR**. This is glutinous with an "i," not an "e," meaning sticky and chewy, not full of gluten. In fact, rice flours are gluten-free. Glutinous rice flour is frequently used in Asian cooking and baking. The most common brand is Erawan, from Thailand, which is what I use. Erawan can be purchased in Asian markets; it comes in clear plastic bags with a green border and lettering.

MOCHIKO is a specific brand of glutinous rice flour. As the name suggests, it is frequently used to make mochi, chewy Japanese rice cakes. The only difference between Mochiko and glutinous rice flour is the type of rice used to make it. Mochiko is made from short-grain Japanese sticky rice, while other brands like Erawan are made from long-grain Thai sticky rice. It's my habit to always use Mochiko when making mochi, but it's interchangeable with glutinous rice flour, so feel free to use either.

POTATO STARCH is a starch extracted from potatoes. Like cornstarch, it can be used to thicken, gel, and give texture to sauces, soups, fillings, and baked goods. Compared to cornstarch it has fewer calories and carbohydrates. It also gels at a lower temperature, meaning it will thicken faster and yield a glossier and more satiny finish.

RICE FLOUR is simply milled rice ground into a flour. It is not the same as glutinous rice flour, as it is made from plain, not sticky, rice. Rice flour can also be used as a thickening agent but is more commonly used to make rice noodles and rice cakes. I use Erawan brand, the clear bag with red writing.

TAPIOCA STARCH, aka **TAPIOCA FLOUR**, is a starch extracted from cassava root. Because of its versatility and indiscernible taste, it is a staple in gluten-free baking. Like other starches, it is a great thickening agent and can also be used to add crispiness and chewiness to baked goods. It is used frequently in Asian cooking for chewy desserts and as a coating on foods before deep frying. It is the main ingredient in tapioca and the larger boba pearls found in your favorite milk teas. I use Erawan brand, the clear bag with blue writing.

WHEAT STARCH is not the same as wheat flour; it is the starch that remains after removing all the proteins and gluten from wheat flour. It has a squeaky consistency, like cornstarch or tapioca starch. Although it goes through processing to remove all the gluten, if you are celiac or gluten-intolerant, I do not suggest you eat it, as it is not considered gluten-free. Wheat starch is used in Asian cooking to make dumpling wrappers, bao, rice rolls, and certain types of noodles. Not all wheat starch is created equal; in other countries, generic wheat starch can be more floury than starchy. I highly recommend purchasing an Asian brand such as Red Lantern, Double Lantern, or Man Sang. I have successfully used all of these brands before.

WHOLE-WHEAT FLOUR is considered healthier than other flours because it is made from 100 percent hard wheat and goes through the least amount of processing. This means it contains higher amounts of fiber, vitamins, minerals, and protein. It can be used to bake an array of breads, cookies, and biscuits, lending a toothsome chew and wheaty flavor. I use King Arthur brand whole-wheat flour.

Spices & Dry Ingredients

AGAR AGAR is a gelling agent that is extracted from seaweed. This colorless, odorless, and tasteless product comes in various forms, including powder, flakes, and sheets. It is used to gel, thicken, and stabilize a variety of foods and is popular throughout Asia as a vegan alternative to gelatin. It sets much more quickly and firmly than gelatin, so depending on what you're making, you may want to opt for gelatin instead. I always use powdered agar agar.

CHINESE CHILI FLAKES, also known as **SICHUAN CHILI FLAKES**, are very similar to the Italian crushed red pepper flakes that New Yorkers love to put on their pizza. The only difference is Italian chilis are roasted before they're crushed, which doesn't yield a color as vibrantly red as the Chinese version.

CHINESE FIVE-SPICE POWDER is a mixture of ground star anise, Sichuan peppercorns, fennel seeds, cloves, and cinnamon. It is often used to season pork and other meats as well as baked goods. It has become so popular that it can be found in the spice aisle of most supermarkets.

COCOA POWDER is commonly available in two types: Dutch-process and natural. Dutch-process cocoa powder is made from cocoa beans that have been washed in an alkaline solution of potassium carbonate, which neutralizes their acidity and yields a darker color and a smoother taste. Natural cocoa powder is untreated, unsweetened cocoa beans ground into powder. I always use Dutch-process cocoa powder for baking and making hot chocolate. I use Cacao Barry extra brute, but you will only find it through baking suppliers. Any Dutch-process cocoa powder like Ghirardelli brand will suffice in these recipes.

CUSTARD POWDER is a thickening agent. When added to dairy and eggs, it forms a custard. Typically comprised of cornstarch, milk powder, and vanilla, it is easily found in Europe, the United Kingdom, and Asia under varying brands. One of the most popular brands that can be found here in the United States is Bird's Custard Powder. To achieve the signature yellow hue found in many Asian baked goods, I use Lion brand custard powder, which originates from Hong Kong; it can be found in some Asian markets or your favorite online marketplace.

FURIKAKE is a Japanese dry seasoning frequently used with rice, vegetables, and fish. It comes in many different blends but most commonly contains seaweed flakes, sesame seeds, bonito (fish) flakes, salt, and sugar. Shake it on top of any dish to deliver an umami punch.

GOCHUGARU is a coarsely ground Korean chili powder and one of the most important ingredients in Korean cuisine. It is made from sun-dried seedless Korean chiles with a mellow heat level that is akin to a jalapeño. The flavor of gochugaru is smoky, slightly fruity, and sweet.

HOJICHA is a Japanese green tea that is made by roasting mature tea leaves, stalks, and stems in a porcelain pot over charcoal. It is reddish-brown in color with a sweet and nutty flavor and very little bitterness. Hojicha is lower in caffeine than other teas and comes in leaf or powder form.

HORLICKS is a sweet malted-drink powder that hails from the United Kingdom and is popular in other Commonwealth countries. Formulated from a mixture of wheat flour, malted wheat, and malted barley, it is typically mixed with warm milk. I use it to add malty flavor to frostings and ganache.

KOSHER SALT is always used in professional kitchens for its larger flake size. No additives, iodine, or sea pollutants are in kosher salt since it is mined on land. It weighs less than table salt, so if you are using a fine table or sea salt in these recipes, halve the amount called for in the ingredient list. I use Diamond Crystal, but if you can't find it, Morton coarse kosher salt works as well.

MATCHA is powdered green tea leaves and comes in different grades. Ceremonial-grade matcha, the highest quality available, uses leaves from the first harvest, yielding a much more vibrant color and sweeter flavor. Culinary-grade matcha uses older leaves, creating a muddier color and more bitter finish. I always use ceremonial-grade matcha in my recipes for the color pop, but it is quite pricey. Culinary-grade will work just fine, but it may not look or taste exactly the same.

MILK POWDER is liquid milk dehydrated into powder form. I use it to add flavor and tenderize bread and other baked goods. It is important to get whole milk powder and not non-fat for these recipes; your results won't be as rich with non-fat. I use Nestle Nido dry whole milk, which can be found in most supermarkets.

OVALTINE, like Horlicks, is a malt-based drink powder popular in the United Kingdom and other Commonwealth countries. This one incorporates the addition of cocoa powder and a ton of essential vitamins and minerals. Usually stirred into warm milk, it tastes like a malted hot chocolate. I use it to add maltiness and a little extra cocoa kick to recipes.

PALM SUGAR is a sweetener made by boiling palm tree sap until it thickens. It is sold in the form of crystallized bricks or pucks. Palm sugar is frequently used as a natural sweetener in Southeast Asia and has a unique taste similar to caramel or smoky butterscotch.

PORK FLOSS is a dehydrated meat product popular in China, Vietnam, and Indonesia. It is made by cooking down marinated pork until the meat completely breaks down. It is shredded and dried, then smashed and cooked again. It becomes so dry that the final texture is similar to that of cotton candy. It is often used as a condiment or in baked goods. I use Kimbo brand, red label. Kimbo also offers a blue label with chunkier floss, but I prefer the finer texture of the red label.

PRESERVED MUSTARD GREENS are made from the stems of Sichuan mustard greens. They are seasoned, dried, and fermented, resulting in a very distinctive flavor: salty, tangy, and a little funky. They can be stirred into soups and stir-fries and pair especially well with pork. I have never seen a label in English for this product. Look for these in the same aisle as other preserved vegetables, called "sui mi ya cai" in Chinese.

RED BEAN PASTE made from sweet red beans ("adzuki" in Japanese) is a very popular ingredient in East Asian sweets. It's one of my favorite flavors, but it's not as popular in the States, as a lot of people can't get past the idea of beans as a dessert. The taste is distinct, like a sweet potato, cocoa, nutty, black bean hybrid. You can find it in the canned fruit aisle at your local Asian market. Make sure to buy one that says "red bean paste" on it. The picture should look like a maroon-colored mashed potato, without any whole beans present.

SICHUAN PEPPERCORNS are dried berries from a prickly ash tree. The taste is very peppery and bitter, with notes of citrus. It's most famous for its mala, the spicy numbing and tingly sensation that it produces on the palate.

STAR ANISE comes from a type of evergreen tree native to China and Vietnam. This star-shaped spice has a sweet licorice flavor and is used all over Asia in savory dishes, desserts, and drinks, such as chai.

THAI STICKY RICE, also known as sweet rice or glutinous rice, is a long-grain rice from Thailand. Very similar to sushi rice, it is starchier than its short-grain Japanese counterpart, which allows it to hold its shape better after cooking. I use Elephant brand glutinous rice.

THAI TEA is a black tea with star anise, cardamom, and tamarind. It usually contains orange food coloring as well, to give it its signature hue. Almost always mixed with sweetened condensed milk or evaporated milk, Thai tea has a delightful flavor reminiscent of vanilla custard and honey, which I channel into my granita.

TOGARASHI is a Japanese chili powder, and there are three different kinds. Shichimi togarashi contains a blend of seven ingredients: chili, sancho pepper, sesame seeds, hemp or poppy seeds, ginger, seaweed, and yuzu. Ichimi togarashi is solely Japanese chili powder, with no other ingredients. Nanami togarashi is much like the shichimi blend but more citrus forward, and it is used mainly on seafood.

TURMERIC is a root related to ginger that is known for its deep golden-orange hue. Used as a natural food coloring, turmeric also possesses powerful antioxidant and anti-inflammatory properties. It is a common ingredient throughout Asia and is probably best known for giving curries their signature golden hue. The taste itself is quite woodsy and earthy, with a spicy bite.

VIETNAMESE CINNAMON (also called **SAIGON CINNA-MON**) is considered the finest varietal of cinnamon. This bark is packed with antioxidants and has a much richer, spicier flavor than regular cinnamon.

VIETNAMESE COFFEE is made by slow-dripping water onto robusta coffee beans over a phin filter directly into a small cup, which typically contains condensed milk. It's a rich and intense mixture unlike anything else. It's crazy delicious. In the tea and coffee aisle of any Asian market you will find an array of instant Vietnamese coffees. I love using these little packets of powder to flavor my desserts.

WHITE RABBIT CANDY is an iconic Chinese milk candy that is toothsome, chewy, and deliciously creamy. Shaped like a Tootsie Roll, White Rabbit candy has gained a huge following in recent years as it has become a symbol of Chinese childhood nostalgia in pop culture. I fold the candies into cookies and pastries and melt them into a Rice Krispie bar–like treat.

YEAST is an organism that helps bread rise by releasing carbon dioxide. When it comes to baking, there are two types: fresh and dry. Fresh yeast comes in the form of a spongy block and crumbles like feta. It is extremely perishable and needs to be stored in the refrigerator. Fresh yeast is a lot harder to come by, especially for the general public, so most people use dry yeast instead. You can use active dry yeast, which needs to be activated in warm liquid prior to mixing, or instant yeast, which is what I use in all my recipes. Instant yeast has the longest shelf life and can be thrown into the mix without pre-activation.

Produce

DRAGON FRUIT, also known as **PITAYA** or **STRAWBERRY PEAR**, is indigenous to southern Mexico and other Central and South American countries along the Pacific coast. It's also cultivated in East and Southeast Asia. This tropical fruit has a beautiful pink shell with spiky green flames and can have white- or fuchsia-colored flesh, speckled with tiny black seeds. Freeze-dried dragon fruit powder is frequently used as a natural food coloring because of its bright pink hue. Many say the fruit tastes like nothing, which I can't really argue against because it is very bland, but still sweet and refreshing.

GARLIC CHIVES are also called **CHINESE CHIVES**. They are longer than the chives you top baked potatoes with and have wider, flatter leaves. They are sometimes sold with the bulbs still attached to the ends. The flavor is much stronger and more garlicky than regular chives. In Asian cooking they are used more as a vegetable than an herb.

JACKFRUIT is native to South and Southeast Asia, where it grows on trees in the form of a giant spiky pod. When cracked open it reveals smaller yellow fruits. When canned in syrup, it has a slight bubblegum taste. Eaten fresh it is slightly sweet, a little bland, and reminiscent of an apple-mango-banana hybrid. Because of its ability to absorb flavors and its shreddy texture, unripened jackfruit is often used in vegetarian and vegan cooking as a meat substitute.

KABOCHA SQUASH, also known as a **JAPANESE PUMPKIN**, is my favorite type of squash. Its forest-green exterior and yellowish-orange flesh resemble an acorn squash. The taste of a kabocha is somewhere between a pumpkin and a sweet potato. It brings moistness, but not wateriness, to cakes, quick breads, cookies, and pie filling.

LYCHEE is native to Southeast Asia. The fruit has a rocky, reddish-pink shell that reveals an opulent rosy-white semi-translucent flesh. *Lee-chee* is the Mandarin pronunciation, whereas *lye-chee* (how I say it) is the Cantonese. Either way, this fruit is delicious and highly fragrant. In the 1990s and 2000s, lychee martinis were all the rage. The taste is refreshing and floral with subtle notes of strawberry.

MANGO is a stone fruit originating from Asia that is now cultivated in most tropical countries. There are over five hundred varieties of mangoes, but Philippine and Champagne are my favorite varieties to use in recipes. Philippine, also known as Carabao or Manila, is held to be the sweetest varietal, with silky, smooth flesh. Another good option is the more common Champagne mango, also called Honey or Ataulfo. These are golden, smaller, flatter, and less fibrous than the rounder greenish mangoes you will usually find in the grocery store.

PANDAN is a tropical plant from Southeast Asia also known as screwpine. Its long, fibrous leaves are frequently tied in a knot and used to flavor both savory and sweet dishes. The taste is grassy, slightly floral, and coconutty, and it lends a beautiful lemon-lime-green color to food. The leaves can sometimes be found fresh in the produce section of your local Asian market or more frequently found in the frozen aisle. There are also two types of pandan extract. Butterfly brand pandan extract looks like food color gel and is very, very strong and saturated. Dragonfly brand pandan essence is a more pleasant translucent green shade, but you will have to use more to achieve the same level of flavor as with Butterfly.

PASSION FRUIT is native to South America but also cultivated and widely used in Asia. The taste is very distinctive, extremely sour, and sweet with some floral notes. Passion fruit can be very expensive, and you will need a lot of them to garner enough juice for a recipe, so a trick is to go to your local Latin market and have a look in the freezer section. There you will find an array of tropical fruit pulp and purées packaged in little baggies for next to nothing.

UBE, also known as purple yam, is like the national food of the Philippines. If you go there, you will know what I mean. Everywhere you turn you will see purple foods and treats. Ube's flavor is like a vanilla marshmallow with a sweet-potato texture, and its bright purple hue is completely natural. It comes in many forms: dehydrated powders, frozen pulps, extracts. Butterfly brand makes an ube extract that is very saturated and very strong, so use with caution.

YUZU is a type of citrus native to East Asia. The zest is frequently used in savory dishes. The juice tastes like a cross between a lemon, mandarin orange, and lime, with a touch of floral. Because of this flavor profile, yuzu lends a distinctive note to pastries.

Fats, Pastes & Liquids

BUTTER. The higher the fat content in butter the better, but these days butter prices are sky high, so I can't really expect everyone to run out and buy the best-quality European-style butter. I do, however, want to make sure everyone uses unsalted butter in their baking. In professional kitchens, both savory and pastry chefs use unsalted butter so we can control the overall flavor and saltiness of our dishes.

CHINESE BACON is cured pork belly that has been marinated in soy sauce, brown sugar, and spices before being air cured. It's absolutely delicious and comes in thicker slabs than regular bacon. You can find it prepackaged in the refrigerated meat section next to the Chinese sausages at your local Asian market.

COCONUT MILK. We all know what coconut milk is, but for Asian cooking and baking using the carton stuff that is on the counter at your local coffee shop is a no-go. Please make sure to get the full-fat coconut milk that comes in cans in the Asian section of the grocery store or your neighborhood Asian market. I use Chaokoh or Aroy-D brand.

GOCHUJANG is a fermented red chili paste that is one of the most popular condiments in Korean cuisine. It is sweet, spicy, and tangy, with a little funk. It comes in red plastic cartons in the dry seasonings aisle, although I have seen it in the refrigerated aisle as well.

HOISIN SAUCE is a thick, dark sauce commonly used in Chinese cooking. It's salty, tangy, sweet, and full of umami. It is sometimes compared to an American barbecue sauce and frequently used as a glaze on meats, alongside Peking duck, or as a condiment for dishes like rice rolls.

KEWPIE is a Japanese mayonnaise. It differs from American mayo in that it is made with only egg yolks instead of whole eggs, and rice vinegar instead of white vinegar. This makes for a richer, sweeter, more custardy and eggy mayo that I use every chance I get.

LARD is the fat of choice in many Latin American countries and throughout Asia. The name alone puts people off because it screams *fat fat fat*! But in some cases, lard really makes or breaks a recipe. Lard is rendered animal fat, usually pork, and comes in a block either on the shelf with the oils or sometimes in the refrigerated section next to the butter and margarine. I use Armour brand Manteca.

MISO PASTE is a Japanese fermented soybean paste that you probably know from miso soup. There are over a thousand different kinds of miso, but in the United States you will primarily find two types: white (shiro) miso or red (AKA) miso. White miso has a sweeter, milder flavor than red miso, which is dark in color, fermented for longer, and has a much stronger aroma.

NONSTICK SPRAY. In professional kitchens we use a lot of nonstick spray, especially in the pastry kitchen. It comes in real handy for everything from greasing bowls to proofing bread, greasing cake pans, or holding down parchment paper on a baking sheet. Probably the most famous brand is Pam. I recommend you keep it as a staple in your pantry.

OYSTER SAUCE is a very common condiment in Asian cuisine. This dark, thick, and viscous sauce is made by cooking down oysters and mixing with sugar, salt, soy sauce, and MSG. The flavor is not so fishy as you would imagine; it's more complex, with deep ocean flavors, extremely salty, sweet, tangy, and umami.

PEANUT SAUCE. Maybe the most common way to indulge in peanut sauce is to use summer rolls or satay as a vehicle, but it can be used in many more applications. Peanut sauce can be found in a jar or bottle, or you can easily make your own by combining peanut butter, soy sauce, rice vinegar, sugar, and some type of chili sauce.

SESAME PASTE. In this book I use Chinese sesame paste, which comes in white and black versions. Unlike tahini, Chinese sesame paste is made from toasted sesame seeds, which produce a darker, nuttier, and richer flavor. If you are unable to find Chinese sesame paste, it won't kill the recipe if you substitute tahini, but note that the taste won't be as strong. Black sesame paste may be harder to come by depending on where you live. It is more easily found in Japanese markets or online.

SHAOXING WINE is a Chinese rice wine that is an essential pantry ingredient if you do a lot of Chinese cooking. Its slight sweetness and acidity add depth to a variety of foods including marinades, fillings, and sauces; it is also frequently used for deglazing the wok or pan. The closest substitute for Shaoxing wine is sherry.

YAKULT is a Japanese sweetened probiotic milk drink. It usually comes in a pack of five little bottles in the refrigerated section next to the yogurt drinks. Yakult was one of my favorites growing up, and it is still one of my favorite flavors. It's tart, tangy, floral, milky, sweet, and super refreshing. It is such an iconic beverage that you may not even have to travel to an Asian market to find it.

Tools & Equipment

Here I have outlined some of the items you will need for a perfect bake.

ACETATE ROLLS, also called **CAKE COLLARS**, are clear strips used around cakes and other desserts to hold them together. They can also be used for making chocolate decorations. These rolls of varying widths can be found at your local baking supply store.

BAMBOO STEAMER. There are plenty of recipes in this book that require a steamer. If you have a metal one, that is fine too, but you may need to wrap a towel around the inside of the lid to prevent any condensation from dripping onto the food. With bamboo steamers you won't have to worry about that, as the bamboo will absorb any moisture and prevent it from dripping. I suggest getting at least a double-decker one. If you don't have a steamer at all, there are plenty of ways to MacGyver one together, which I have highlighted in the recipes.

BENCH SCRAPER. This tool is a baker's best friend. It looks like a metal rectangle with a wooden or silicone handle. We use bench scrapers for everything from chopping up blocks of butter to portioning dough to scraping down work surfaces.

BLOW TORCH. If you love a good toasty meringue like I do, you should definitely have one of these on hand. I have the big blue one that looks like a fire extinguisher, but they come in little sizes, too, for brûléeing and more precise actions. Pro tip: They're usually cheaper at a hardware store.

BOWL SCRAPER. Usually made of polypropylene or silicone, these half-moon shaped tools are perfectly flexible for scraping out every last bit of batter or dough from the bowl.

CHINESE ROLLING PIN. My latest favorite tool is perfect for rolling out dumpling skins. They are a lot like regular rolling pins but shorter and thinner. I find they work better for most home projects because you have more control.

DIGITAL SCALE. Professional bakers and pastry chefs rely on the metric system to measure all their ingredients for the utmost accuracy. Why is it better than measuring in cups? Well, for example, I can measure 1 cup of flour and it will weigh 150 g, while somebody else's cup of flour might weigh 140 g. Ten grams may not sound like a huge difference, but when it gets up to 2 or 3 cups, the difference gets bigger, and that can make a huge difference in the outcome of your final product. I wrote these recipes using the metric system, so to get the most accurate outcome I highly suggest weighing the ingredients using a digital kitchen scale.

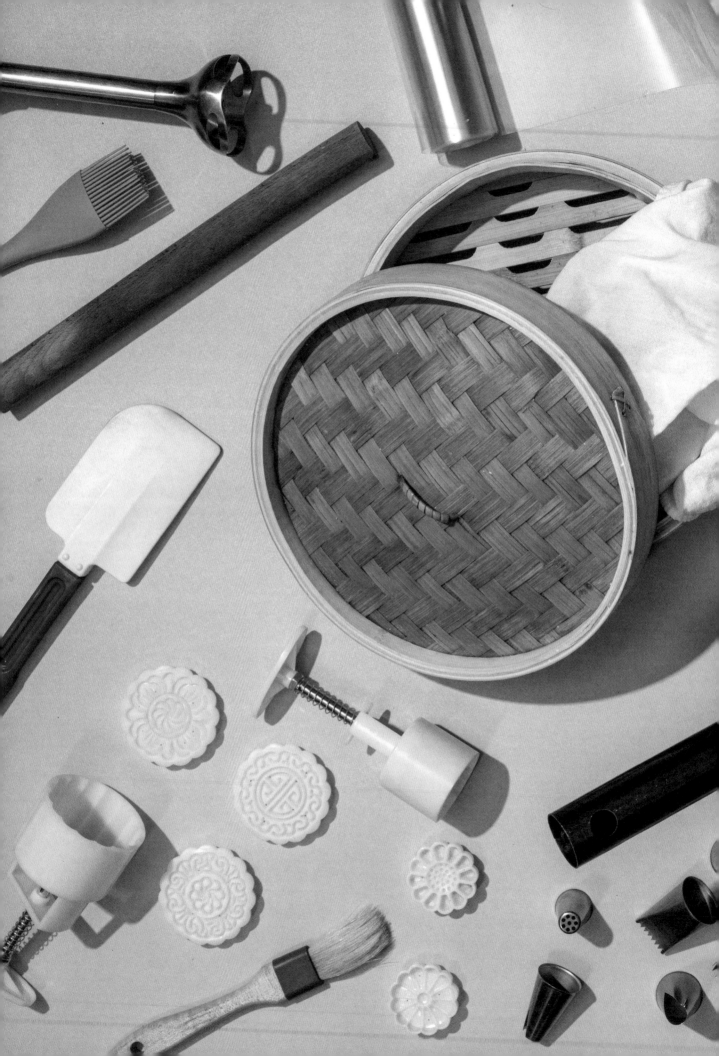

IMMERSION BLENDER. Also called a stick blender or beurre mixer, this is one of the most underrated tools, in my opinion. I use this so often for emulsifying everything from savory sauces to ganaches.

LOAF PANS. A standard loaf pan in the United States is 8½ by 4½ by 2½ in [21.5 by 11 by 6 cm]. There is also a Pullman loaf pan, which has squared, rather than sloped, sides and a lid, which results in a long rectangular loaf that looks like a stick of butter. Pullman pans come in different sizes from 4 in [10 cm] cubes to 16 in [40.5 cm] long and skinny rectangles.

MOONCAKE MOLDS look like presses, with interchangeable pieces embossed with ornate designs to stamp out the little cakes. They're used to make mooncakes during the mid-autumn festival; I also like to use them for pressing cookies. You may find them in an Asian market in September, but the easiest way is to buy them from your favorite online marketplace, where you will find the most options for sizes and shapes.

OFFSET SPATULAS are an essential tool for baking and pastry. They have flexible blades bent at an angle, which makes them ideal for smoothing and spreading. If you do a lot of baking, you should have a small and a large one.

PIPING BAGS/TIPS. I am always using piping bags. If you keep a roll of them on deck, I guarantee you will use them more than you think. I always use disposable piping bags and prefer 18 to 20 in [46 to 51 cm] sizes. It's also great to have a collection of piping tips around. And forget about the little dinky tips that come in a set; unless you are decorating cookies, those are pretty useless. A good start would be to get a set of round and star tips, Ateco brand 801–809 and 821–829. In this book we also use St. Honoré tips, Ateco 880–883.

RUBBER SPATULA. You probably already have rubber spatulas, but do you have a red-handled one? Those are my favorite. They are high heat–resistant, and the handle is super stiff, which makes stirring and folding much easier and more ergonomic. The absolute best are made by Volrath.

STAND MIXER. If you do a lot of baking, a stand mixer really is a must. I have a fancy-pants Waring Commercial one at home, but any 6- to 8-quart mixer will work. A handheld electric mixer will work for most things except bread.

STANDARD BAKING SHEET. Is your cupboard filled with fifty different-sized baking sheets and pans? Might I suggest starting a collection of standard-sized sheet pans? These pans are the only ones chefs use in the kitchen, and they come in sizes from ⅛ sheet to full sheet. Quarter sheets and half sheets are the sizes you'll use most at home. These pans have a 1 in [2.5 cm] lip, which is great for baking layer cakes and keeping things uniform in height, and the standardized sizes are awesome for stacking. You can also find parchment paper, aluminum foil, and wax paper precut to fit precisely within these trays.

STEAMER CLOTH is a cloth, usually made of muslin, that is used to line a steamer basket so the food doesn't stick to it. The breathability of the fabric allows the steam to perfectly penetrate the food. You can find them in packs of varying sizes in the housewares section of your local Asian market. In a pinch you can substitute a thin muslin or cotton tea towel, but make sure it doesn't smell like laundry detergent unless that's what you want your food to taste like.

STRAIGHT-EDGE RULER. If you are an avid baker, this common and underrated tool should be a part of your tool set to ensure consistency. I use mine literally all the time! Just make sure to get a stainless steel one for sanitary purposes.

A **THERMOMETER** is another essential tool. I used to be intimidated by any recipe that required taking something to a specific temperature, but really, it's nothing to be scared of. You have a couple options: candy or digital. Candy thermometers are great, but they break all the time, and that's just how it is, so I suggest having a backup, just in case. Digital thermometers are great, too, but make sure to get one with a long prong so the plastic reader part doesn't melt. Whichever you choose, you should calibrate it by measuring the temp of boiling water. If it doesn't read 212°F [100°C] at boiling point, then you should keep the difference in mind when making these recipes.

BAO

My closest friends will tell you how much I loathe the term "bao buns." It's truly one of my biggest pet peeves. It's like saying "chai tea" or "spaghetti pasta"—redundant and unnecessary. A bao is already a bun, but most people don't know that *bao* translates to much more than that. In Chinese, the most common definition is a steamed bun, but it can also refer to a dumpling, a treasure, the act of wrapping something, or bread in general.

This chapter contains recipes that fall under all of those definitions. You will find everything from steamed and baked breads to deep-fried treasures and laminated parcels, from donuts to French toast. Don't be intimidated by the daunting task of baking bread; with detailed instructions down to the minute, you will be able to recreate each of these recipes with finesse and prowess.

Shokupan

Japanese Milk Bread

Shokupan, or Japanese milk bread, is one of the most common recipes in Asian baking. Pick out any bread in an Asian bakery, and chances are it has a milk bread base. Asian milk bread recipes start with a tang zhong, a roux-like mixture of milk or water and flour that is cooked on the stovetop until it resembles a paste. The paste is cooled and then added to the main dough to give shokupan its signature soft and feathery texture. Because of its versatility, I use this recipe often, and you will see it referenced many times throughout the book. This tender and bouncy milk bread will stay fresh on your counter for days, or up to a week in the refrigerator, and freezes extremely well.

YIELD: Makes twelve 1¾ oz [50 g] buns or 1 standard loaf

TANG ZHONG

¼ cup [60 ml] whole milk

3 Tbsp bread flour

DOUGH

1¾ cups [265 g] bread flour

3 Tbsp granulated sugar

2 large eggs

2 Tbsp heavy cream

2 Tbsp whole milk

2 tsp whole milk powder

1¾ tsp instant yeast

1 tsp kosher salt

2 Tbsp unsalted butter, cubed, at room temperature

EGG WASH

1 large egg

2 large egg yolks

1 Tbsp whole milk

¼ tsp kosher salt

1   To make the tang zhong, in a small pot, add the **milk**, ¼ cup [60 ml] of water, and the **bread flour** and whisk to combine. Bring to a boil over medium-high heat and continue whisking until a thick paste forms, 3 to 5 minutes. Transfer the tang zhong to a small bowl and let cool to room temperature.

2   To make the dough, in the bowl of a stand mixer fitted with the dough hook attachment, add the **bread flour**, ⅓ cup [90 g] of the tang zhong (discard the rest), the **sugar**, **eggs, cream, milk, milk powder, yeast**, and **salt**. Mix on low speed for 3 minutes, then increase the speed to medium and mix for an additional 7 minutes.

3   With the mixer running, add the **butter** several cubes at a time, allowing the dough to come back together before adding more. Once all the butter has been added, continue to mix on medium speed until the butter is fully incorporated, 2 minutes more. The dough will be sticky.

4   Grease a large bowl with nonstick spray or vegetable oil. Place the dough into the bowl and cover with a tea towel. Let it proof until doubled in size, 1½ to 2 hours.

5   Punch the dough down and turn it out onto a lightly floured work surface. Flatten the dough with your hands to release any remaining gas bubbles.

6   For buns, line two baking sheets with parchment paper. Divide the dough into twelve equal [50 g] pieces. Take one portion of the dough and flatten it using the palm of your hand. Fold the edges inward and pinch it shut; it should kind of look like a dumpling. Turn the ball of dough seam-side down onto your work surface and cup your hand over it between the edge of your hand and the fleshy part under your thumb. Roll in a circular motion, trying to keep the seam constantly on the surface, until the dough piece forms a tight ball. Repeat with the remaining dough pieces and place on the prepared baking sheet.

cont'd

Cover each sheet loosely with a tea towel and proof again until doubled in size, about 1 hour. Proceed to step 9.

7   For a Pullman loaf, spray a 9 by 4 by 4 in [23 by 10 by 10 cm] Pullman loaf pan and underside of the lid generously with nonstick spray, making sure to coat the corners. Remove about ½ cup [100 g] of dough and discard, or shape into two buns to munch. Roll the dough out into a rectangular shape approximately the same length as the loaf pan. With the long side facing you, roll the dough away from you, into a log, and pinch the seam to seal. Place the dough log seam-side down into the pan, pressing it in to fill the corners. Slide the lid on, leaving a 1 in [2.5 cm] opening to see the progress. Proof until the dough barely touches the underside of the lid, about 1 hour. Proceed to step 10.

8   For a regular loaf, grease the inside of an 8½ by 4½ in [21.5 by 11 cm] loaf pan. Divide the dough into thirds. Roll each portion into a rectangle, about 4 in [10 cm] wide and ½ in [13 mm] thick. With the 4 in side facing you, roll each piece away from you as you would a cinnamon roll. Pinch the seam shut, repeat with the other portions, and place all three logs side by side into the loaf pan, with the 4 in side parallel to the 4 in side of the pan and the seams at the bottom. Cover with a tea towel and let the dough proof until doubled in size, about 1 hour. Proceed to step 9.

9   To make the egg wash, in a small bowl, add the **egg, egg yolks, milk,** and **salt** and whisk until smooth. Pour through a fine-mesh sieve to strain out any solid bits.

10 Preheat the oven to 375°F [190°C]. If making buns or a regular loaf, brush with two coats of the egg wash (do not egg wash the Pullman loaf). For buns, bake until deep amber brown, 15 to 20 minutes. For loaves, bake until the internal temperature measures 200°F [95°C], 40 to 45 minutes.

11 If you made buns, let them cool on the baking sheets or wire racks. If you made a Pullman loaf, carefully slide the lid off and flip to unmold onto a wire rack to cool. If you made a regular loaf, allow it to cool in the pan before slicing and eating.

Pro Tips & Storage

- Shokupan can be kept in zip-top bags or airtight containers for up to 4 days at room temperature, 1 week in the refrigerator, or 3 months in the freezer.

- Cut the loaf into thin slices for egg salad, tuna salad, or chicken salad sandwiches. Cut the loaf into thicker slices for delicious breakfast toasts or French toast.

- Enjoy a piece of toast with some Banana Jam (page 117), Strawberry-Rose Confit (page 101), Hojicha Milk Jam (page 101), or Kaya Jam (page 107).

- Dress up the buns by sprinkling with garnishes of your choice after egg washing and before baking: white or black sesame seeds, everything bagel seasoning, flakes or strips of seaweed, and so on.

- Garnish the buns after baking with some flaky Maldon sea salt or with a thin spread of Kewpie followed by a dunk into pork floss.

Gochujang Pizza Rolls

When I was a kid, the only thing I wanted to eat was Totino's pizza rolls. My favorite was the supreme flavor (which, devastatingly, they don't make anymore): tomato sauce, sausage, green peppers, and cheese. To this day I still love pizza rolls, and when I thought about making my own version, I took the assignment very literally. Why not take shokupan and shape it like cinnamon rolls? I could picture spirals of soft bread filled with a sticky and spicy tomato sauce, thanks to the addition of gochujang, a Korean sweet chili paste. Once I brought the recipe to life, I almost gave myself vertigo by staring into the beautiful coils of mortadella, soppressata, and salame. I hope you will be just as mesmerized after making these.

YIELD: Makes 9 rolls

1 recipe Shokupan (page 35)

3 Tbsp tomato paste

2 Tbsp gochujang

2 Tbsp heavy cream

2 cups [160 g] shredded low-moisture mozzarella

6 slices mortadella

12 slices soppressata

6 slices herbed salame

1 recipe Egg Wash (page 35)

Fresh basil, for garnish (optional)

1 Make the **shokupan** up to step 5. Line a baking sheet with parchment paper.

2 On a lightly floured surface, roll out the dough to a 10 by 13 in [25 by 33 cm] rectangle. Transfer the dough to the prepared baking sheet, cover loosely with plastic wrap, and place it in the refrigerator for 15 minutes.

3 Meanwhile, in a small mixing bowl, make the sauce by whisking the **tomato paste, gochujang,** and **cream** together.

4 Place the dough back onto your floured work surface with the long side facing you. Spread the sauce over the dough, edge to edge, and sprinkle with the **mozzarella.** Arrange the **mortadella** slices to cover the cheese, then the **soppressata** over the mortadella, and finally the **salame** on top.

5 With the long side facing you, carefully roll up the dough into a log as you would cinnamon rolls. Place the log back onto the prepared baking sheet, cover loosely with plastic wrap, and place it back in the refrigerator for 15 minutes. (Chilling the dough will create cleaner cuts.)

6 Grease a 9 in [23 cm] square baking pan with nonstick spray, oil, or butter. Remove the log from the refrigerator and, using a serrated knife, cut it into nine equal pieces, about 1½ in [4 cm] thick. With the spiral side of a roll facing up, pull the tail of the dough and tuck it under. Repeat with the other portions. Place the rolls into the greased pan, three-across, three-down. Cover

loosely with plastic wrap and proof until doubled in size (there should still be some space between the rolls), about 1 hour.

7 Preheat the oven to 375°F [190°C] and make the **egg wash.** Brush the tops of the rolls with two coats of egg wash, then place in the oven and bake until medium amber brown, 30 to 35 minutes.

8 Remove from the oven and allow to cool completely in the pan. Garnish with **basil,** if desired.

Pro Tips & Storage

- The rolls can be kept in zip-top bags or airtight containers for up to 1 week in the refrigerator or 3 months in the freezer.

- Substitute your favorite cured meats, such as prosciutto, pepperoni, pancetta, bacon, Spanish chorizo, and so on. The possibilities are endless.

- Add other toppings on top of the cheese like minced garlic, sliced onions, cooked Italian sausage, or whatever you normally like on your pizzas.

Char Siu Carnitas Bolo Bao
Baked Chinese BBQ Shredded Pork Buns with Bolo Top

Two of the most well-known Chinese baked goods are char siu bao (barbecue pork buns) and bolo bao (pineapple buns). Of the two, bolo bao were always my favorite; the name comes from the iconic yellow crackly cookie top that resembles the rind of a pineapple. I fill these with my take on Chinese-barbecued pork, which is roasted carnitas-style. The delicately sweet and flaky bolo topping is a dream paired with the bold and juicy flavors from the char siu carnitas. If you prefer a plain bolo bao to take with your morning milk tea or coffee, simply omit the filling.

YIELD: Makes 12 bao

CHAR SIU CARNITAS

2 lb [910 g] boneless pork shoulder or pork butt, cut into 1 in [2.5 cm] chunks

4 garlic cloves, smashed

2 Tbsp vegetable oil

½ tsp kosher salt

½ tsp ground white pepper

3 Tbsp granulated sugar

2 Tbsp honey

2 Tbsp soy sauce

2 Tbsp hoisin sauce

1 Tbsp oyster sauce

1 Tbsp Shaoxing wine

1 Tbsp dark brown sugar

1 tsp sesame oil

½ tsp Chinese five-spice powder

1 recipe Shokupan (page 35)

BOLO TOPPING

½ cup [113 g] unsalted butter, cubed, at room temperature

¾ cup [150 g] granulated sugar

2 large egg yolks

1 cup + 2 Tbsp [170 g] all-purpose flour

¼ cup [30 g] custard powder

½ tsp baking powder

½ tsp kosher salt

1 recipe Egg Wash (page 35)

1. To make the carnitas, preheat the oven to 325°F [165°C]. In a 9 in [23 cm] square baking dish or roasting pan, combine the **pork, garlic, vegetable oil, salt,** and **white pepper.** Toss to coat evenly. Cover the pan tightly with foil and roast for 1½ hours.

2. Remove the pork from the oven, reserve ¾ cup of the juices and drain the rest.

3. In a 2 cup [480 ml] liquid measuring cup whisk the **sugar, honey, soy sauce, hoisin sauce, oyster sauce, Shaoxing wine, brown sugar, sesame oil,** and **five-spice powder.** Pour over the pork in the pan along with the reserved juices and toss to coat. Re-cover the pan with foil and roast for 1 hour more until the pork is cooked through, about half of the sauce has been absorbed, and the meat is tender and easily shreddable.

4. Remove the foil. Using two forks, shred the pork and mix. The sauce in the pan will absorb into the meat as it sets.

5. Allow the carnitas to cool in the pan at room temperature for 1 hour, then refrigerate for at least 1 hour. If not using immediately, store in an airtight container in the refrigerator.

6. Make the **shokupan** up to step 5.

cont'd

7 Line two 13 by 17 in [33 by 43 cm] baking sheets with parchment paper. Portion out the dough into twelve equal [50 g] pieces. Lightly dust your work surface with flour. Take one portion of the dough and flatten it using the palm of your hand. Add a heaping tablespoon or two of carnitas to the center of the dough. Fold all the edges inward and pinch shut; it should loosely resemble a dumpling. Turn it seam-side down onto your work surface and roll into a tight ball. Repeat with the remaining dough pieces, placing six buns on each sheet. Cover each sheet loosely with a tea towel and let them proof until doubled in size, about 1 hour.

8 Meanwhile, make the bolo topping. In the bowl of a stand mixer fitted with the paddle attachment, combine the **butter** and **sugar**. Mix on low speed, moving up to medium speed until light and fluffy, about 2 minutes.

9 Scrape down the sides and bottom of the bowl and add the **egg yolks** one at a time, allowing the mixture to come back together before adding the next. Scrape down the sides of the bowl and mix on medium speed until fully incorporated, about 1 minute.

10 Scrape down the bowl again and add the **flour, custard powder, baking powder,** and **salt**. Mix until it just comes together into a shaggy ball of dough, about 30 seconds.

11 Divide the dough in half and place one portion in between two sheets of parchment paper measuring roughly 12 by 16 in [30.5 by 40.5 cm] each. Roll out the dough into a thin layer, ⅛ in [3 mm] thick, mimicking the shape of the parchment. Place the sheet of rolled dough onto a baking sheet and refrigerate until ready to use. Repeat with the other portion.

12 Preheat the oven to 375°F [190°C] and make the **egg wash**.

13 Remove the sheets of bolo dough from the refrigerator, peel off one piece of parchment paper, gently lay it back onto the dough, flip the whole thing onto your work surface, and peel off the other piece of parchment. Use a 3½ in [9 cm] circle cookie cutter to cut out twelve discs. Save the scraps and reroll them between two sheets of parchment paper to cut more discs. Repeat until the dough runs out.

14 Egg wash the tops of the buns and the bolo discs. Place one disc on top of each bun and bake until golden brown, 25 to 30 minutes, rotating halfway through baking. Allow the buns to cool on the baking sheets or on wire racks.

Pro Tips & Storage

- Bao can be stored in zip-top bags or airtight containers for up to 1 day at room temperature, 4 days in the refrigerator, or 3 months in the freezer.

- Premade and leftover carnitas can be stored in an airtight container for up to 4 days in the refrigerator or 3 months in the freezer.

- There will be extra char siu carnitas. Use it as an alternate filling for the Ham Sui Gok (page 51), Sheng Jian Bao (page 49), LPB (page 65), or Pan-Fried Mochi (page 55); add a few dabs along with the scallions when rolling the Scallion Roti Canai (page 60); or use it for tacos, fried rice, or omelets.

Pork Floss and Scallion Focaccia

Yuk sung, or pork floss, has a light and fluffy texture similar to cotton candy. It might sound odd, but trust me, it's delicious. It is used as a topping or filling in countless dishes and is also a popular ingredient in baked goods. Go to any Chinese bakery and you will see an array of buns and pastries either filled or topped with it.

If you want a more traditional yuk sung bao, you can bake Shokupan (page 35) buns, lather some Kewpie on top, and then dunk it like a donut into pork floss. However, in this recipe, I bake it into focaccia with some scallions. It has a crispy exterior and chewy, springy interior with a nice open crumb, and the result is the most addictive umami bite.

YIELD: Makes 6 to 8 servings

2½ cups [375 g] bread flour

1 tsp instant yeast

½ cup [120 ml] extra-virgin olive oil

1½ tsp kosher salt

¾ cup [30 g] pork floss

4 scallions, finely chopped

2 tsp Maldon salt

1   In the bowl of a stand mixer fitted with the dough hook attachment, combine the flour, 1 cup [240 ml] of tepid water, and the yeast. Mix on low speed until combined, 1 minute.

2   Add ¼ cup [60 ml] of tepid water and 1 Tbsp of the olive oil. Start on medium-low speed and mix until it stops splashing around, about 3 minutes. Add the salt, increase the speed to medium, and mix until smooth and silky, 7 minutes more. Grease an 8 in [20 cm] square baking pan with 1 Tbsp of the olive oil. Turn the dough out into the pan, cover it with a tea towel, and let it rest for 1 hour.

3   Sprinkle about 2 Tbsp of the pork floss on top of the dough. Make a coil fold: Wet your hands and reach under the dough from the middle and pull it upward until it releases from the pan. Then roll it forward, folding it on top of itself. Rotate the pan 90 degrees and repeat. Wet your hands as needed if the dough sticks. Cover with the towel and let it rest for 30 minutes.

4   Repeat step 3 two more times. By now, the dough should have rested for a total of 2½ hours with three sets of coil folds. Add ¼ cup [60 ml] of the olive oil to a 9½ by 13 in [24 by 33 cm] baking pan. Use your fingertips to spread the olive oil around, making sure the bottom of the pan is evenly coated. Wet your hands and carefully transfer the dough to the oiled pan.

5   Wet your hands again and pick up the dough, gently pulling and stretching, forming it to the shape of the pan. Use your fingertips to press and dimple the dough all over, making sure the dough gets into all the edges and corners of the pan. Let it proof until puffy and doubled in size (1 in [2.5 cm] high), about 1 hour. Drizzle 1 Tbsp of the olive oil over the top, then sprinkle with the rest of the pork floss and the scallions.

6   Wet your fingertips and then gently press and dimple the dough. It should create different-sized bubbles and the dough should jiggle. Allow it to rest for 30 minutes.

7   Preheat the oven to 475°F [245°C]. Drizzle the dough with the remaining 1 Tbsp of olive oil and sprinkle with the Maldon salt. Wet your fingertips, and flick and splash some water over the top. Bake until deep amber brown, 25 to 30 minutes. Allow to cool completely in the pan at room temperature.

cont'd

Pro Tips & Storage

- The focaccia can be kept in zip-top bags or double plastic wrapped for up to 3 days at room temperature, 1 week refrigerated, or 3 months in the freezer. If refrigerated, bring the bread to room temperature for half an hour or warm in the toaster oven. If frozen, transfer to the refrigerator the night before, then warm as above, or heat in the microwave at 60 percent power for 20 seconds, then transfer to the toaster oven to bake until toasted on top and warmed through, 3 to 4 minutes.

- The focaccia dough can be made up to 2 days in advance. As a bonus, aging the dough allows it to develop a deeper flavor. To do so, make the recipe up to step 5. Drizzle the top with more olive oil and use your fingers to smear it around. Double wrap the entire baking pan in plastic wrap and place it in the refrigerator for up to 2 days. When you are ready to bake, remove the plastic wrap and let the dough come to room temperature for about 2 hours. At this point the dough should be loose enough to continue to step 6. If the dough is not stretchy enough yet, allow it to sit for another half hour or so before proceeding.

- You can treat this like any focaccia recipe. Try topping it with dollops of the corn mixture from Kimchi–Corn Cheese Filling (page 55) or Char Siu Carnitas (page 40) or with more traditional toppings like rosemary, tomatoes, caramelized onions, cheese, and so on.

- Make a delicious breakfast sandwich by slicing a piece of focaccia in half, toasting it, and adding fried or scrambled eggs.

- Serve a piece of focaccia with spaghetti and Hong Kong Bolognese (page 51).

Dan Dan Sheng Jian Bao
Pan-Fried Dan Dan Bao

Sheng jian bao are small pan-fried buns hailing from Shanghai, usually filled with juicy pork. It's not considered a dumpling because it uses mantou, the same kind of dough as steamed bao, creating a fluffy exterior that balances out the crispy fried bottom. Because the exterior is so durable, a saucy filling is welcome.

Dan dan noodles are an iconic staple of Sichuan cuisine and, coincidentally, my partner's favorite. The first time I introduced him to creamy, spicy, and uber umami dan dan noods, I thought his head was going to explode from excitement. There are many ways to make and serve these noodles, but the main ingredients remain the same: crispy ground pork with a sauce made of sesame paste and chili oil over a bed of freshly boiled noodles. This recipe marries the two beloved dishes.

YIELD: Makes sixteen ¾ oz [20 g] bao

BASIC MANTOU

1½ cups [190 g] cake flour

¼ cup + 3 Tbsp [105 ml] whole milk

1 Tbsp granulated sugar

2 tsp vegetable oil

1 tsp instant yeast

¼ tsp kosher salt

DAN DAN FILLING

1 Tbsp vegetable oil

1 tsp sesame oil

8 oz [230 g] ground pork

3 Tbsp Chinese sesame paste or tahini

3 Tbsp soy sauce

3 garlic cloves, minced

2 tsp hoisin sauce

2 tsp Shaoxing wine

½ tsp granulated sugar

½ tsp Chinese five-spice powder

¼ tsp ground white pepper

1 Tbsp preserved mustard greens

2 Tbsp Chili Crisp (page 76)
or store-bought chili crisp, plus more
for garnish (optional)

2 to 4 Tbsp [30 to 60 ml] vegetable oil

2 scallions, green and white parts finely chopped (optional)

1 Tbsp roasted black sesame seeds (optional)

1. To make the mantou, in the bowl of a stand mixer fitted with the dough hook attachment, combine the flour, milk, sugar, oil, yeast, and salt. Knead on low speed until it comes together, about 1 minute, then increase to medium speed for 9 minutes more. The dough should look very smooth.

2. Lightly grease a medium mixing bowl with some vegetable oil. Turn the dough out into the bowl and cover with plastic wrap. Allow the dough to proof until doubled in size, about 1 hour.

3. Meanwhile, make the dan dan filling. In a medium sauté pan, heat the vegetable oil and sesame oil over medium-high heat. Add the pork to the pan and fry, breaking it up as it cooks, until lightly browned and cooked through, 3 to 5 minutes.

4. In a small bowl, whisk together the sesame paste, soy sauce, garlic, 1 Tbsp of water, the hoisin sauce, Shaoxing wine, and sugar.

5. When the pork is cooked through, lower the heat to medium, add the five-spice powder, white pepper, and preserved mustard greens to the pork, and stir to combine. Pour in the sauce mixture and stir until all the meat is coated and the sauce has thickened.

6. Transfer to a bowl and stir in the chili crisp. Set aside to cool on the counter for 15 minutes before covering with plastic wrap and placing in the refrigerator to chill.

7. Punch the dough down and place it on a lightly floured work surface. Roll it into a log and portion it into sixteen equal [20 g] pieces. Cover the pieces with plastic wrap so they don't dry out.

cont'd

8 On a lightly floured work surface, shape a piece of dough into a ball and then flatten it into a 3 in [7.5 cm] circle using the palm of your hand. Place about 1 Tbsp of the filling in the center of the dough. (If you have one, a 1 Tbsp cookie scoop works really well here.)

9 Make a cup with your nondominant hand and place the dough with filling onto your four fingers. Use your thumb to hold the filling down. Work your way around the edges making eight pleats and pinch them all together to seal. It should look like a sack with a drawstring top. Place on a parchment-lined baking sheet and cover loosely with plastic wrap. Repeat with the remaining dough pieces and filling.

10 Allow the buns to proof until 50 percent larger, about 45 minutes.

11 In a large pan, heat 2 Tbsp of the **vegetable oil** over medium-low heat and place the buns into the pan. Do not overcrowd the pan, as the bao will get bigger as they cook. Work in two batches if you have to. Fry until lightly browned on the bottom, about 2 minutes. If they are getting brown too fast, lower the heat.

12 Add ⅓ cup [80 ml] of water to the pan, cover, and continue to cook until the water has evaporated, the buns are fluffy and cooked through, and the bottoms are browned and crisp, about 8 minutes more.

13 Place the buns on a plate and garnish with the **scallions** and **sesame seeds**, if desired, and more chili crisp, if desired.

Pro Tips & Storage

- Leftover cooked buns can be stored in an airtight container for up to 3 days in the refrigerator.

- Try swapping out the dan dan filling for Char Siu Carnitas (page 40), Hong Kong Bolognese (page 51), or Kimchi–Corn Cheese Filling (page 55).

- Preserved mustard greens have a very distinct flavor. If you can't find them in your local Asian market or online, you can substitute some finely chopped scallions, which taste nothing like it but are green and have a flavor that will work with the dish.

- If you want to make these as steamed bao, follow the recipe up to step 10. Place each bun on a little square of parchment paper and then steam in a bamboo steamer or metal steamer with a tea towel tied around the underside of the lid (to catch any condensation) for 10 minutes. It is imperative to bring the water to a rolling boil before placing any buns in the steamer.

- You can turn this into a noodle dish by making the sauce in steps 3 through 6. Boil noodles following the package directions, add 3 Tbsp of water from the boiled noodles to the pan, and simmer for 3 minutes. Place some Chili Crisp (page 76) at the bottom of your bowl, then top with noodles and finally the sauce.

Hong Kong Bolognese Ham Sui Gok

Fried Glutinous Rice Dumplings Filled with Hong Kong Bolognese

Yes, Hong Kong Bolognese sauce is a thing! When I was a kid, whenever we visited Hong Kong, I insisted we go to The Spaghetti House, an Italian restaurant of sorts but where the sauces were made the Asian way: more gravyish, sometimes stir fried, and usually made using bottled ingredients like ketchup and Worcestershire sauce.

When I lived in Italy, I tasted my first arancini, deep-fried risotto balls that are typically stuffed with cheese and sauce. I have combined both these memories into my own version of one of my favorite dim sum dishes, ham sui gok, deep-fried glutinous rice dumplings. If you don't feel like fussing with making the wrappers, just make the sauce and serve it over a bowl of spaghetti for an umami bomb that you won't want to end.

YIELD: Makes 15 dumplings

HONG KONG BOLOGNESE

2 Tbsp vegetable oil

1 small yellow onion, finely chopped

3 garlic cloves, minced

8 oz [230 g] lean ground beef

2 Tbsp ketchup

2 Tbsp tomato paste

½ Tbsp oyster sauce

1 cup [240 ml] low-sodium chicken stock

½ cup green peas, shelled, fresh or frozen

1 Tbsp low-sodium soy sauce

1 Tbsp granulated sugar

1 tsp Worcestershire sauce

1 tsp kosher salt

½ tsp ground white pepper

HAM SUI GOK (DUMPLING WRAPPERS)

½ cup [70 g] wheat starch

⅓ cup [80 ml] boiling water

¼ cup [50 g] granulated sugar

½ tsp kosher salt

2 cups [220 g] glutinous rice flour

3 Tbsp lard, unsalted butter, or shortening

6 cups [1.4 L] vegetable oil

1   To make the Hong Kong Bolognese, in a wok or large frying pan, heat the **vegetable oil** over medium-high heat and sauté the **onion** and **garlic** for 1 to 2 minutes. Add the **ground beef** and continue to cook, breaking it up and stirring until browned, about 2 minutes more. Drain the liquid from the beef.

2   Stir in the **ketchup, tomato paste,** and **oyster sauce** and cook for another 2 minutes. Stir in the **chicken stock** and bring to a boil.

3   Lower the heat to a low simmer and add the **peas, soy sauce, sugar, Worcestershire sauce, salt,** and **white pepper.** Continue to cook until thickened, 10 to 15 minutes.

4   Allow to cool for at least 30 minutes at room temperature before placing in an airtight container to chill in the refrigerator for at least 2 hours.

5   Meanwhile, make the ham sui gok dumpling wrappers. In a small mixing bowl, add the **wheat starch** and **boiling water.** Mix using chopsticks

or a fork until it comes together in a shaggy ball. Turn the dough out onto a floured work surface and knead by hand until smooth, 2 to 3 minutes. Cover with plastic wrap and set aside.

6   In a medium pot, bring ⅔ cup [160 ml] of water, the **sugar,** and **salt** to a boil. Remove from the heat and add the **glutinous rice flour.** Stir using a wooden spoon, smashing the dough against the sides of the pot, smearing it to help it come together into a rough ball.

7   In the bowl of a stand mixer fitted with the dough hook attachment, add the wheat starch dough, the glutinous rice flour dough, and the **lard.** Knead on medium speed until smooth and stretchy, about 3 minutes. If the dough has not totally come together, stop the mixer, scrape down the sides, and gather the dough, giving it a couple folds onto itself by hand, then place it back in the mixer to knead for another 2 minutes.

cont'd

8 Form the dough into a long log and wrap it in plastic wrap. Allow the dough to rest on the counter for 1 hour.

9 In a large heavy-bottomed pot over high heat, bring the 6 cups of **vegetable oil** to 330°F [165°C].

10 Segment the dough log into fifteen equal [35 g] pieces and roll each piece into a ball. Using the palm of your hand, flatten each ball into a disc. Using a rolling pin, roll it out into a 3 in [7.5 cm] circle about ¼ in [6 mm] thick.

11 Holding a wrapper in the palm of your nondominant hand, place 1½ Tbsp of the chilled Hong Kong Bolognese in the center. Fold the wrapper in half and pinch the edges to seal. Place it onto a parchment-lined baking sheet or large plate seam-side up, flattening the bottom. The shape should vaguely resemble a football. Repeat with the rest. Loosely cover with plastic wrap so they don't dry out.

12 Working in batches, place 3 to 5 dumplings into the hot oil without overcrowding the pot. Fry until deep golden brown and cooked through, 10 to 12 minutes. Remove from the oil using tongs or a spider and allow to cool on a wire rack or baking sheet lined with paper towels.

Pro Tips & Storage

- The dumplings should be eaten the day they are fried.

- Dumplings can be preassembled and stored in a single layer on a parchment-lined baking sheet, wrapped in plastic wrap, for up to 3 days in the refrigerator or 3 months in the freezer.

- The Hong Kong Bolognese can be made ahead and stored in an airtight container for up to 4 days in the refrigerator or 3 months in the freezer.

- Keep an eye on the oil temperature while frying, especially if you are frying straight from the refrigerator or freezer. It is normal for the temperature to dip once you put them in, but if it doesn't rise back up, you will need to regulate it. You want to keep it as close to 330°F [165°C] as possible.

- If you are frying straight from the refrigerator or freezer, the dumplings will take longer to cook.

- Try making the Hong Kong Bolognese and serving it with spaghetti and a fried egg on top.

- Try swapping out the filling for Char Siu Carnitas (page 40), Dan Dan Filling (page 49), Kimchi–Corn Cheese Filling (page 55), or Chinese Bacon, Egg & Chive Filling (page 57).

Kimchi & Corn Cheese Pan-Fried Mochi

The inspiration behind this dish comes from two of my favorite Korean dishes: corn cheese and tteokbokki, spicy stir-fried rice cakes. Korean corn cheese technically falls into the category of anju, dishes that are served with alcohol, but is also frequently served as a side dish at Korean BBQ restaurants. I usually finish it before the meat even hits the table. It's made of corn, mayo, and seasonings, topped with a mountain of shredded cheese, and cooked under the broiler until brûléed and gooey. It's the perfect comfort food. When I make tteokbokki at home I like to add cheese to cut through the spiciness, and when I make corn cheese at home, I like to add kimchi. So why not combine all three iconic Korean foods into one dish?

YIELD: Makes seven 1¾ oz [50 g] pieces

PAN-FRIED MOCHI DOUGH

2 cups [220 g] Mochiko or glutinous rice flour

2 tsp granulated sugar

¼ tsp kosher salt

2 tsp vegetable oil

KIMCHI–CORN CHEESE FILLING

1 Tbsp Kewpie or regular mayo

½ Tbsp unsalted butter, melted

2 tsp gochujang

1 tsp granulated sugar

1⅓ cup [200 g] fresh, frozen, or canned and drained corn

½ cup [50 g] shredded low-moisture mozzarella

2 Tbsp roughly chopped kimchi

2 garlic cloves, minced

2 to 4 Tbsp [30 to 60 ml] vegetable oil

2 scallions, finely sliced, for garnish (optional)

1   To make the mochi dough, in a medium mixing bowl, add the Mochiko. In a small pot, bring ½ cup + 1 Tbsp [135 ml] of water, the sugar, and the salt to a rolling boil.

2   As soon as it boils, remove the pot from the heat and pour it into the bowl with the Mochiko. Using a pair of chopsticks or a fork, stir the dough until it won't stir anymore. It should look like a shaggy lump of dough. Cover the bowl tightly in plastic wrap and allow to sit for 5 minutes.

3   Remove the plastic wrap and add the vegetable oil. Knead the dough by hand in the bowl until the oil is incorporated, then transfer it onto your work surface and knead until smooth, about 5 minutes. Roll it into a log and wrap in plastic wrap. Allow the dough to rest for 30 minutes.

4   Meanwhile, make the kimchi–corn cheese filling. In a small mixing bowl, whisk together the Kewpie, butter, gochujang, and sugar until combined.

5   Add the corn, mozzarella, kimchi, and garlic and mix well. Set aside.

6   Divide the dough into seven equal [50 g] pieces. Lightly grease your work surface with some vegetable oil. Roll a portion into a ball and flatten it into a 3½ in [9 cm] disc using the palm of your hand. Keep the rest covered in plastic wrap so it doesn't dry out.

7   Place about 3 Tbsp of filling into the center of a dough circle. Gather all the edges together and pinch to seal into a ball shape. Make sure everything is completely sealed so it doesn't ooze out when you fry them. Flip the ball over so the seam side is down and lightly flatten the ball into a hockey puck shape using the palm of your hand. Repeat with the rest. Keep the mochi covered with plastic wrap while you are shaping so the dough doesn't dry out.

cont'd

8 Preheat a large pan over medium heat. Add 2 Tbsp of oil and place the mochi bao in the pan, in batches if necessary, making sure to keep space between them so they don't stick together. Cover the pan and fry until golden brown, 3 to 4 minutes on each side. (If you don't cover the pan, they won't cook all the way through before burning.) Add more oil if necessary. If they are turning brown too fast, lower the heat a little.

9 Place the mochi bao on a plate and garnish with sliced **scallions**, if desired. Allow to cool slightly before serving. The inside will be very hot.

Pro Tips & Storage

- I recommend eating these the day they are fried, but if you have leftovers, you can store them in an airtight container for up to 3 days in the refrigerator.

- They can be assembled in advance and stored uncooked in a single layer on a parchment-lined baking sheet or plate, wrapped in plastic wrap, for up to 3 days in the refrigerator or 3 months in the freezer. Cooking times will be longer if you are frying them straight from the fridge or freezer.

- Not a fan of spicy? Leave out the kimchi and gochujang; it will still taste great.

- Try substituting this filling for Chinese Bacon, Egg & Chive Filling (page 57), Wild Mushroom–Boursin Filling (page 65), Black Sesame Filling (page 82), or Chestnut Filling (page 87).

- You could also go more traditional and fill the mochi bao with red bean paste.

Breakfast Crystal Bao

Har gow, Chinese shrimp dumplings, had always been one of my favorite dim sum dishes, not because of the shrimp inside, but rather the wrapper, or the "skin," as I call it. Visually, I loved how transparent it was and how cute all the pleats looked stacked on top of each other. Texturally, I loved the buoyancy of the dough.

One day, I was thinking about another Chinese dish: egg and chive pockets, which traditionally have vermicelli noodles in them, and how I wished I could feel and taste the noodles more. That led me to thinking how it would be more effective for my personal palate if the noodle was on the outside like a har gow, only bigger, so it feels more like a bao. And that's how this dish came about, my friends.

YIELD: Makes eight 1 oz [26 g] bao

CRYSTAL WRAPPER

½ cup + 1 Tbsp [100 g] potato starch

3 Tbsp tapioca flour

¼ tsp kosher salt

1½ tsp vegetable oil

CHINESE BACON, EGG & CHIVE FILLING

5 large eggs

½ cup [35 g] finely chopped Chinese garlic chives

1 Tbsp heavy cream or whole milk

½ tsp kosher salt

¼ tsp ground white pepper

1 Tbsp vegetable oil

½ cup [85 g] Chinese bacon cut into ¼ in [6 mm] cubes

Chili Crisp (page 76) or store-bought chili crisp, to serve (optional)

Soy sauce, to serve (optional)

1 To make the crystal wrapper, in a medium mixing bowl, add the potato starch and tapioca flour.

2 In a small pot, bring ½ cup [120 ml] of water and the salt to a boil.

As soon as it boils, take it off the heat and pour it into the bowl with the potato starch.

3 Using a pair of chopsticks or a fork, stir the dough together until it looks like a shaggy mass. Cover the bowl with plastic wrap and let it sit for 5 minutes.

4 Add the vegetable oil to the dough and knead by hand until smooth, bouncy, and not sticky, about 5 minutes. Place it in an oiled bowl with plastic wrap directly on the dough and allow to rest for 30 minutes.

5 Meanwhile, to make the filling, in a medium mixing bowl, whisk together the eggs, chives, cream, salt, and white pepper.

6 In a medium sauté pan, heat the vegetable oil over medium-high heat. Add the Chinese bacon and cook until browned on the edges, about 2 minutes. Add the egg mixture, lower the heat to medium-low, and scramble the eggs. Cook until just done. Transfer the scrambled

eggs to a bowl and allow to cool completely.

7 Cut eight 3 in [7.5 cm] squares of parchment paper.

8 Roll the dough into an 8 in [20 cm] log. Cut at every inch [2.5 cm] to make eight equal [26 g] pieces. Lightly grease your work surface with a tiny bit of vegetable oil. Flatten each piece into a disc and roll it out into a 5 in [13 cm] circle as thin as possible without breaking. The dough should be thin enough that you can see through it.

9 Place about 3 Tbsp of filling in the center of a dough circle. Imagine a triangle shape within the circle, one point on top and two points at the bottom. Fold the edges of the circle up at your imagined points to form a triangle shape and pinch to seal. Place the dumpling on top of a square of parchment and repeat with the rest.

10 Prepare a two-basket steamer and bring the water to a rolling boil.

cont'd

If you don't have a steamer set, fill a wok or large pot with 1 to 2 inches of water, then place the steamer baskets inside. Make sure there is at least an inch of space between the bottom of the basket and the water. If you don't have two baskets, work in two batches. Place the bao into the baskets without overcrowding. Turn the heat down to medium to keep it at a simmer and steam for 10 minutes.

11 Remove the steamer baskets from the water and allow to sit, covered, for 5 minutes before serving. The skins will become transparent as the dumplings cool a little. Serve with **chili crisp** or **soy sauce**, if desired.

Pro Tips & Storage

- Leftover cooked crystal bao can be stored in an airtight container for up to 3 days in the refrigerator.

- Uncooked crystal bao can be preassembled and stored on a parchment-lined plate wrapped tightly in plastic wrap for up to 3 days in the refrigerator. Freeze them flat in a single layer on a parchment-lined baking sheet or plate for at least 2 hours, before transferring them to a zip-top bag for up to 3 months. This will prevent them from sticking together.

- If you can't find Chinese bacon, you can substitute pork belly, lardons, pancetta, or thick-cut bacon.

- They can be steamed straight from the refrigerator or freezer; it will take a few minutes longer.

- Try filling these wrappers with Char Siu Carnitas (page 40), Dan Dan Filling (page 49), Hong Kong Bolognese (page 51), or Wild Mushroom–Boursin Filling (page 65).

Scallion Roti Canai
Scallion Laminated Flatbread

My mom used to make jook, Chinese congee, every weekend. While delicious, the real star of the show was the scallion pancakes that she made to go with it. In recent years I've become increasingly obsessed with making the perfect scallion pancake. Unfortunately, and fortunately, I never realized my goal because as I worked my recipe over and over trying to achieve as many flaky layers as possible, it ended up evolving into a roti canai instead.

Roti canai is a laminated flatbread hailing from Malaysia and in other parts of Southeast Asia. It was once named best street food in the world by TasteAtlas, surprising no one. Compared to a scallion pancake, roti canai is puffier and shreddier—especially delicious when it's filled with minced scallions.

YIELD: Makes five 3½ oz [100 g] pieces

2 cups [300 g] all-purpose flour

2 Tbsp sweetened condensed milk

1 tsp kosher salt

3 Tbsp vegetable oil, plus more for shaping and frying

8 scallions, finely minced

1 Tbsp kosher salt

1 In the bowl of a stand mixer fitted with the dough hook attachment, combine the **flour**, ¾ cup [180 ml] of water, the **condensed milk**, and the **salt**.

2 Knead on low speed for 1 minute, then increase to medium speed and mix for 4 minutes more. Scrape down the sides and bottom of the bowl and mix until it forms a ball and is tacky but not sticky, 5 minutes more.

3 Turn the dough out onto a lightly floured work surface, cover with plastic wrap, and let it rest for 30 minutes.

4 Pour the **vegetable oil** into an 8 in [20 cm] square dish or baking pan. Divide the dough into five equal [100 g] pieces and form each one into a ball. Take a ball of dough and roll it around in the oiled dish to completely coat. Repeat with the rest. Cover the dish or pan tightly with plastic wrap and let it rest in a cool, dark place overnight, at least 8 to 12 hours.

5 Lightly grease your work surface with a little vegetable oil. Something like a marble countertop or a stainless-steel surface will work best. Take one ball of dough and flatten it. Use your fingers and palms to gently push the dough, spreading it across your work surface. You can also pick up the edges and gently stretch it out as if you were fluffing a bed sheet. Stretch it into a large rectangular shape as thin as possible without it tearing, about 15 by 20 in [38 by 51 cm]. You should be able to see through the dough.

6 Pour about 1 tsp of vegetable oil over the dough. Use your fingers to dab it and spread it around. Sprinkle a fifth of the minced **scallions** on top and season with ¼ tsp of the **salt**.

7 With the long side facing you, pick up the top edge and lightly flop it over to meet the center. Pick up the bottom edge and lightly flop it over to meet the center. Then fold it in half lengthwise and loosely scrunch it together. Air pockets are good in this case, so when you are folding the dough do not smooth it out or pat it down.

8 Pick up the scrunched dough and gently stretch it apart. Holding it vertically, allow the end to rest on the surface and drape the dough around and around like a coiled snake. Tuck the tail under and repeat with the rest. Cover with plastic wrap and allow the dough to rest for 30 minutes.

cont'd

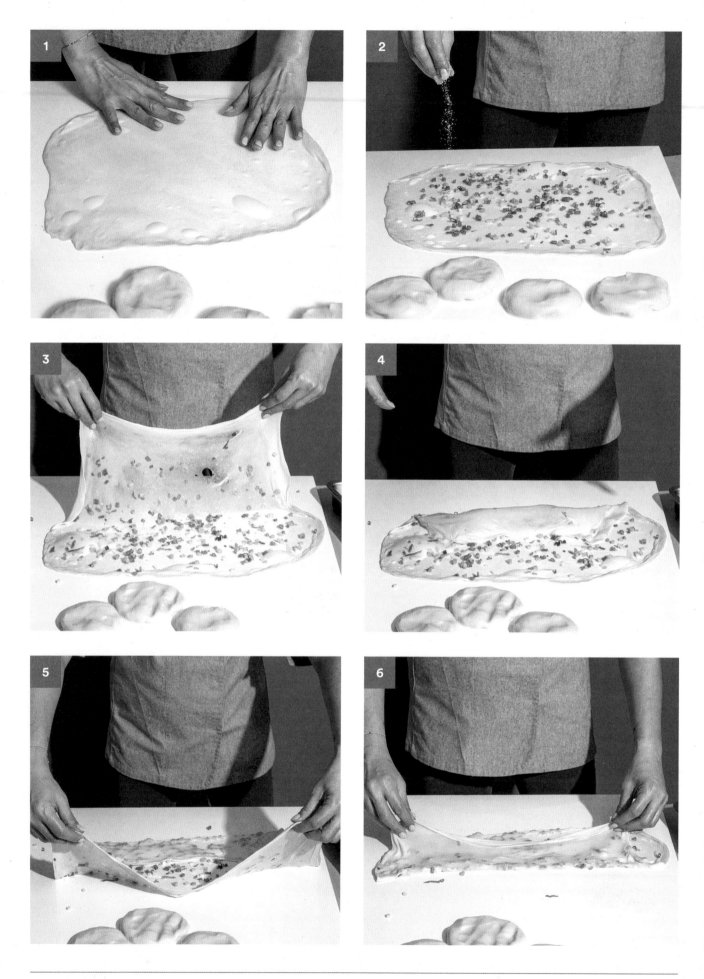

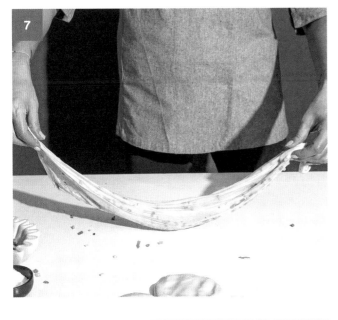

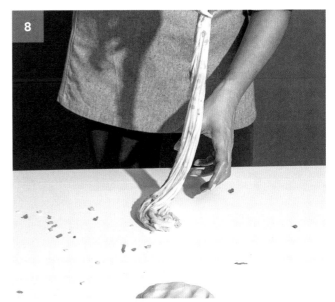

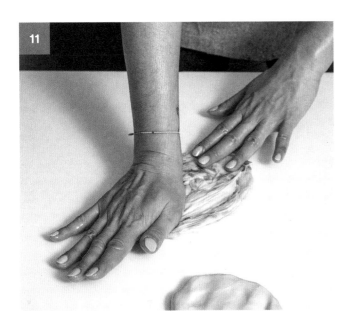

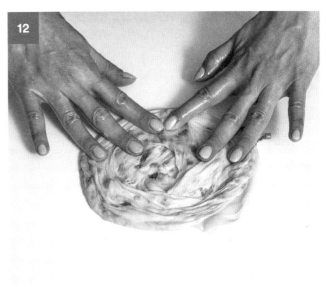

cont'd

9 Take one roti and flatten it, then spread it out using the palm of your hand to an 8 in [20 cm] circle. It should be about ⅛ in [3 mm] thick. Preheat a large frying pan over medium heat.

10 Add 1 tsp of vegetable oil to the preheated pan and swirl it around. Place the roti in the pan. Fry until browned, 3 to 4 minutes on each side. While one is cooking, shape another roti. Repeat with the remaining dough.

11 Take the roti off the heat and allow to cool for a minute. With each roti lying flat on a surface and your hands on either side, clap your hands together, fluffing up the roti and revealing the layers. Rotate the roti and clap again to puff. Serve warm.

Pro Tips & Storage

- Cooked roti canai are best eaten the day they are fried.

- The greased dough balls can be made in advance and kept for up to 3 days in the refrigerator. Allow the dough to sit at room temperature for 2 hours before shaping.

- Shaped roti can be stacked with two pieces of parchment or wax paper in between each one and stored in a zip-top bag or airtight container for up to 3 months in the freezer.

- Try leaving out the scallions and adding minced garlic instead. You can also substitute Chinese chives. Serve alongside your favorite curry or eat it on its own.

Wild Mushroom–Boursin LPB
Chinese Puff Pastry Filled with Wild Mushrooms & Boursin

LPB is my abbreviation for lo pau bang, or "wife cake" in Cantonese (sometimes also referred to as a sweetheart cake or marriage pie). Made of a sou dough, Chinese puff pastry, it is typically encased around a sweet winter melon, almond paste, sesame paste, or red bean filling. One of the primary differences between Chinese puff pastry and traditional French puff pastry is the addition of flour with the fat that is being laminated, which gives it a sturdier and almost crumbly texture. The method of laminating is different as well: rather than folding the layers of dough, sou is rolled up and then coiled. I made this recipe 26 times, trying every kind and combination of fat, varying ratios, folds, rolls, etc., until I finally arrived at this version.

YIELD: Makes 6 LPB

BASIC SOU (CHINESE PUFF PASTRY)

Water Dough

1 cup [150 g] all-purpose flour

2 Tbsp vegetable oil

1 tsp granulated sugar

½ tsp kosher salt

Oil Dough

4½ Tbsp [60 g] margarine, unsalted butter, vegetable oil, or lard

½ cup [75 g] all-purpose flour

WILD MUSHROOM–BOURSIN FILLING

2 Tbsp unsalted butter

8 oz [230 g] mixed mushrooms, such as shiitake, oyster, shimeji, chanterelle, and trumpet, cleaned and roughly chopped

3 garlic cloves, minced

1 Tbsp fresh thyme leaves

1 tsp kosher salt

½ tsp ground black pepper

½ cup [115 g] Boursin cheese

1 recipe Egg Wash (page 35)

Maldon salt, for finishing (optional)

Thyme sprigs, for garnish (optional)

1 To make the basic sou, start with the water dough. In the bowl of a stand mixer fitted with the dough hook attachment, combine the flour, ¼ cup [60 ml] of water, the vegetable oil, sugar, and salt. Mix on low speed for 1 minute, then increase to medium speed and knead until smooth, 4 minutes more. You can also knead the dough by hand; it will take about double the time. Roll the dough into a log, wrap in plastic wrap, and refrigerate for 30 minutes.

2 To make the oil dough, in a small pot, melt the margarine until it just starts to boil. Remove from the heat, add the flour, and stir until smooth and combined. (If using oil, cook it longer, until it turns into a paste.) Transfer the dough to a bowl and cover loosely with plastic wrap. Allow it to rest at room temperature for 30 minutes, but do not let it cool too much or it will be crumbly and hard to work with.

3 Meanwhile, make the mushroom filling. In a sauté pan, melt the butter over medium-high heat. Add the mushrooms and garlic. Cook for 2 to 3 minutes, stirring occasionally. Add the thyme, salt, and pepper, and lower the heat to medium. Sauté until cooked through and browned, about 2 minutes more. Transfer to a bowl and set aside.

4 Preheat the oven to 375°F [190°C] and line a 13 by 17 in [33 by 43 cm] baking sheet with parchment paper.

5 Place the water dough on a lightly floured surface and cut it into six equal [40 g] pieces. Roll the oil dough into a log and portion it into six equal [20 g] pieces. Keep both the doughs loosely covered with plastic wrap to prevent them from drying out.

6 Form the water dough pieces into balls and roll the oil dough pieces into balls.

cont'd

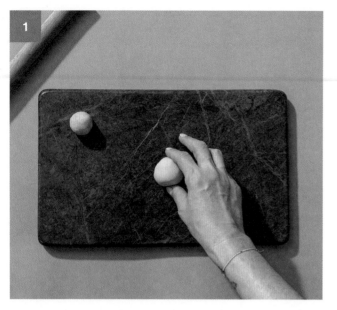

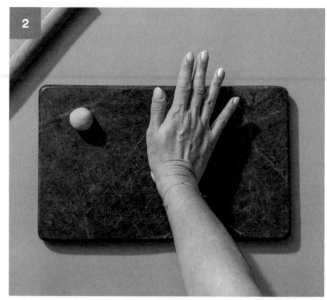

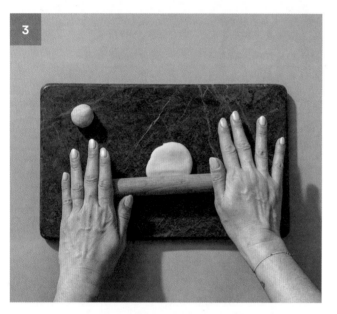

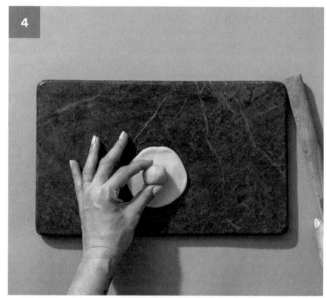

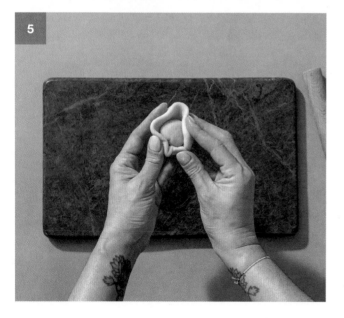

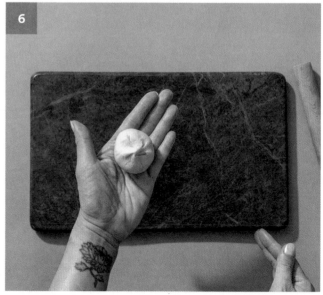

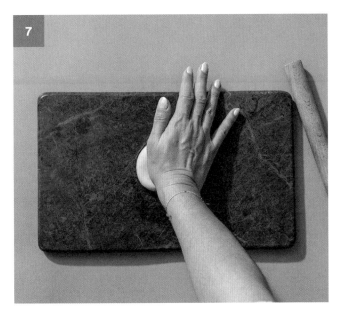

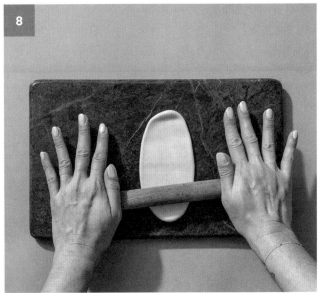

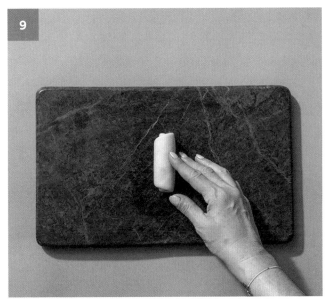

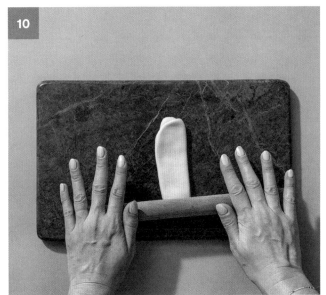

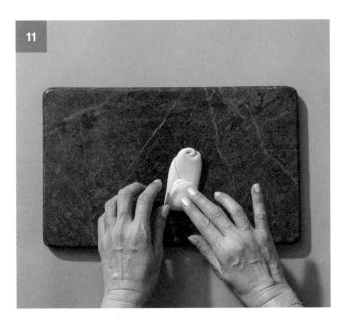

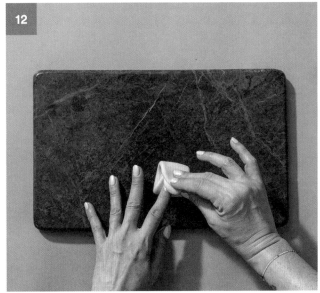

cont'd

BAO   CAKES & DESSERTS   SNACKS

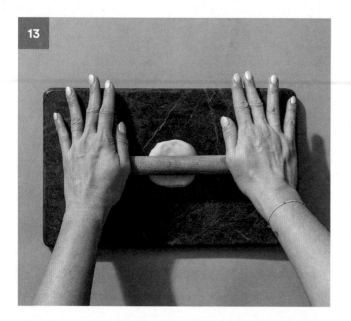

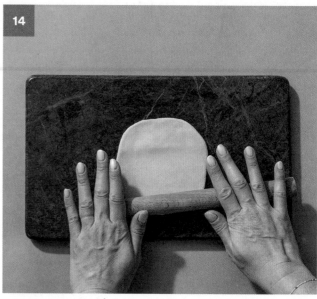

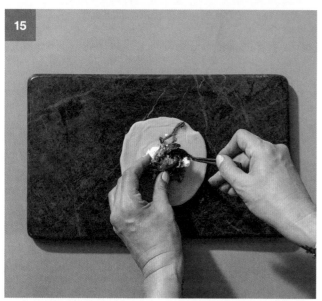

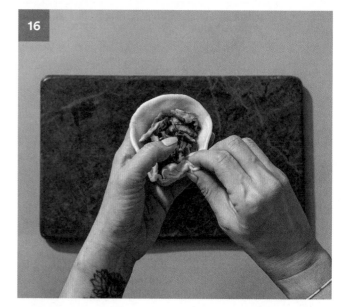

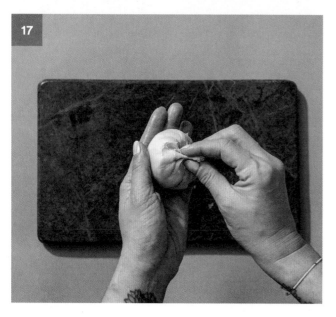

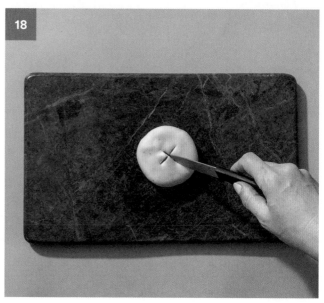

cont'd

7   Take one piece of the water dough, flatten it with the palm of your hand, and roll it out with a rolling pin to a 3½ in [9 cm] disc. Place a ball of the oil dough in the center and wrap the water dough around it, pinching the seams to seal, creating a larger ball of dough. Repeat with the rest.

8   Take the first ball of dough you formed, flatten it with the palm of your hand, and roll it out to a long oval shape about 6 in [15 cm] long and ⅛ in [3 mm] thick. Roll it up like a cinnamon roll. Repeat with the rest.

9   Take the first roll formed, lay it vertically on your work surface, then flatten it. Using a rolling pin, roll it out vertically into a rectangular shape about 5 by 2½ in [13 by 6 cm]. Fold it into thirds so it looks more like a square. Repeat with the rest.

10 Take the first square formed and flatten it, roll it out as best you can into a 5 in [13 cm] circular shape, about ⅛ in [3 mm] thick. Place 1 Tbsp of the **Boursin** in the center, then top with 2½ Tbsp of the mushroom filling. Gather the edges together, forming a ball, and pinch to seal. Use scissors to cut off any extra dough. Place the ball seam-side down and flatten into a disc using the palm of your hand. Place on the prepared baking sheet and repeat with the rest.

11 Brush the top of each LPB with two coats of **egg wash**. Using a paring knife, cut two slits in the top of each like a cross. Bake until golden brown, 30 to 35 minutes.

Pro Tips & Storage

- LPB are best eaten the day they are baked but can be stored in a zip-top bag or airtight container for up to 3 days in the refrigerator or 3 months in the freezer.

- Unbaked LPB can be shaped in advance and frozen in a single layer for 2 hours before being transferred to a zip-top bag or airtight container and stored for up to 3 months.

- The mushroom filling can be made in advance and stored in an airtight container for up to 3 days in the refrigerator.

- You'll probably find the most mushroom varieties in an Asian market. They also come dehydrated, which will work too if you can't find fresh. Just rehydrate them and proceed as normal.

- If you don't live near an Asian market, go to your local fancy market where they should have cartons of mushroom medleys.

- Try filling the LPB with Char Siu Carnitas (page 40), Dan Dan Filling (page 49), Hong Kong Bolognese (page 51), Kimchi–Corn Cheese Filling (page 55), Chinese Bacon, Egg & Chive Filling (page 57), Black Sesame Filling (page 82), Chestnut Filling (page 87), Cherry Pie Filling (page 94), or Coconut Filling (page 109).

Kabocha Galette

Miso Kabocha, Caramelized Onions & Chili Crisp Ricotta on Chinese Puff Pastry

In my younger years, I remember always wanting the "orange one" out of the mixed tempura basket. Decades passed before I learned it was really called kabocha, a Japanese squash that tastes like a pumpkin–sweet potato hybrid. One day, I wanted to make a potato galette, but thought how tasty it would be with kabocha instead—glazed with honey and miso, then baked in a shell made of sou (Chinese puff pastry), topped with caramelized onions and ricotta, and finished with a generous drizzle of my homemade chili crisp. So many flavors, dimensions, and textures for a perfect savory bite.

YIELD: Makes one 8 in [20 cm] galette

KABOCHA GALETTE

1 recipe Basic Sou (page 65)

Half a small kabocha squash (about 10 oz [275 g]), seeded

1 Tbsp white miso

1 Tbsp honey

1 Tbsp soy sauce

2 tsp rice vinegar

2 tsp extra-virgin olive oil

1 tsp sesame oil

CARAMELIZED ONIONS

1 medium sweet onion

1 Tbsp extra-virgin olive oil

1 Tbsp unsalted butter

½ tsp kosher salt

¼ tsp ground black pepper

1 cup [240 g] whole milk ricotta

1 Tbsp Chili Crisp (page 76) or store-bought chili crisp, to drizzle (optional)

1   Make the **Basic Sou** up to step 2. In step 1, after kneading, shape the dough into a flat square instead of a log.

2   On a lightly floured surface, roll the water dough into a 5 by 9 in [13 by 23 cm] rectangle, with the long side facing you, about ½ in [13 mm] thick. Take the oil dough and form it into a 4 in [10 cm] square, also ½ in [13 mm] thick, in the center of the water dough rectangle. Fold both sides of the water dough over the oil dough block to meet in the center. Pinch the seam to seal. Pinch the top seam together and the bottom seam together so the oil dough block is completely enclosed within the water dough.

3   Using a rolling pin, roll the block out up and down, until it is about ½ in [13 mm] thick. Starting from the bottom, use your fingers to roll the dough upward like a cinnamon roll. Rotate the log 90 degrees and flatten it using the palm of your hand.

4   Using a rolling pin, roll the dough out up and down to a rectangle ½ in [13 mm] thick. Fold the bottom edge upward into a third, then the top edge downward over it. Wrap the dough with plastic wrap and place in the refrigerator to rest for 30 minutes.

5   Meanwhile, cut the kabocha into thirteen wedge slices, each ¼ in [6 mm] thick.

6   In a medium mixing bowl, whisk together the miso, honey, soy sauce, rice vinegar, olive oil, and sesame oil until smooth. Add the kabocha slices and toss to coat. Set aside to marinate while you roll out the dough.

7   Preheat the oven to 375°F [190°C]. Place the dough on a lightly floured work surface and roll it out to a 12 in [30.5 cm] circle, ⅛ in [3 mm] thick. Gently fold the dough in half, pick it up, and transfer it to an 8 in [20 cm] tart ring. Lightly drape the dough in the center and press it up the sides without pulling. Using a paring knife, trim off any excess. If you don't have a tart ring, you can follow the next step and fold the edges over for a more rustic galette shape.

cont'd

8 Place each slice of kabocha starting from the center and fanning outward to touch the edge, forming a pinwheel shape. Discard any excess marinade. Place in the oven and bake until the crust is golden brown and the kabocha is cooked through, 25 to 30 minutes. Remove from the oven and place on a wire rack to cool in the pan.

9 To make the caramelized onions, while the galette is baking, cut the **onion** in half lengthwise, then cut each half into ¼ in [6 mm] slices. In a large sauté pan over medium heat, preheat the **olive oil** and **butter**, then add the onions. Cook, stirring occasionally, until browned and caramelized, 10 to 15 minutes. Season the onions with the **salt** and **pepper**, transfer to a bowl, and set aside.

10 Once the galette has cooled completely, remove it from the pan. Place it on a serving plate and fill the empty spaces with the caramelized onions and dollops of the **ricotta**. Drizzle the **chili crisp** over the top, if desired, and serve.

Pro Tips & Storage

- This is best eaten the day it is baked, but leftovers can be wrapped in aluminum foil or stored in an airtight container for up to 3 days in the refrigerator.

- The sou dough can be wrapped in plastic wrap and stored for up to 2 days in advance in the refrigerator.

- Try substituting goat cheese, Boursin, or farmer's cheese for the ricotta. Add fresh herbs or scallions if you like.

- Acorn squash, butternut squash, sweet potato, regular potato, or pumpkin can be substituted for the kabocha squash.

cont'd

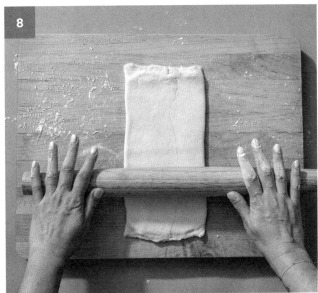

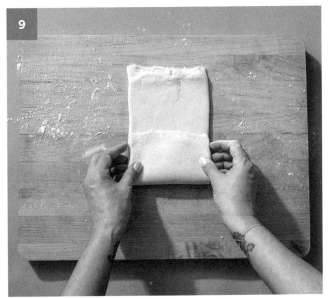

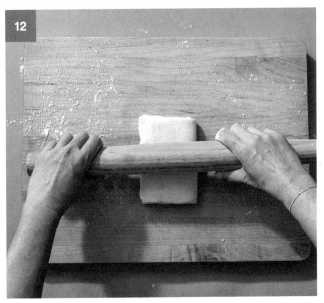

Chili Crisp

Chili crisp or oil is a staple in every Chinese household. Growing up, we had at least five different kinds at all times. Every weekend my mom would make some variation of noodle soup and/or dumplings, and the best part was making our own personal dipping sauce to go with it. I would line the jars up like little soldiers on the counter, open every jar, and whiff them one by one, questioning which aroma matched my feelings that day.

I put chili crisp on everything from noodles to soup to cheese; I find it opens your taste buds and allows more flavors to meld together. It adds texture and, obviously, spice. Making your own may seem intimidating at first, but it's very easy and comes together in about 30 minutes.

YIELD: Makes 2 cups

1½ cups [360 ml] vegetable oil

3 garlic cloves, crushed

3 slices ginger (about 1 Tbsp)

2 scallions, cut into 3 in [7.5 cm] pieces

1 shallot, halved

3 star anise pods

2 bay leaves

½ cup [45 g] crushed Sichuan chili flakes

¼ cup [25 g] gochugaru

1 Tbsp Sichuan peppercorns, crushed with a mortar and pestle

2 tsp kosher salt

1 tsp granulated sugar

1 In a small pot, add the **vegetable oil, garlic, ginger, scallions, shallot, star anise,** and **bay leaves.** Heat over medium-low heat until the oil starts to bubble, about 10 minutes. Lower the heat and continue to cook until the scallions are browned, about 20 minutes.

2 In a small mixing bowl, stir together the Sichuan chili flakes, gochugaru, Sichuan peppercorns, salt, and sugar.

3 Strain the oil and pour it back into the pot. Discard the aromatics. Bring the oil to 325°F [165°C] over high heat. Remove from the heat and carefully add about half of the chili flake mixture to the oil. It will spatter and bubble.

4 Once it stops spattering, carefully add the rest of the chili flake mixture and whisk until the sugar is dissolved and everything is well combined.

5 Allow to sit at room temperature until warm before transferring to a sanitized glass jar.

Pro Tips & Storage

- The chili crisp can be kept in a sanitized glass jar in a cool, dark place for up to 1 month at room temperature or 6 months in the refrigerator. Make sure to allow the chili crisp to cool to room temperature before placing in the fridge.

- Some people like to add additional aromatics like cinnamon sticks or cardamom. Feel free to adjust, add, or take away according to your personal taste.

- Try drizzling this chili crisp on Pork Floss and Scallion Focaccia (page 45), Dan Dan Sheng Jian Bao (page 49), Hong Kong Bolognese Ham Sui Gok (page 51), Breakfast Crystal Bao (page 57), Scallion Roti Canai (page 60), Kabocha Galette (page 71), avocado toast, eggs, cheese, and, if you're feeling feisty, ice cream!

Sweet Corn Custard Bao

Steamed Bao with Sweet Corn Custard Filling

During a family trip to the Philippines, my sister and I discovered mais con yelo, a shaved ice dessert layered with corn, condensed milk, and sometimes corn flakes. We were totally obsessed. It was toothsome, refreshing, and light—a perfect example of how corn is one of those special ingredients that is just as good in savory applications as it is in sweet. To highlight its versatility, I crafted a steamed bao filled with sweet corn custard, and then of course I had to make it into a corn shape because things that look like things are . . . ADORABLE. But don't let that intimidate you from making this recipe. It's easy to shape, but if you're not feeling it, you can skip it and just shape it into a normal bun.

YIELD: Makes 7 bao

CORN CUSTARD

1⅔ cups [250 g] fresh or frozen corn kernels

2 cups [480 ml] whole milk

1 large egg

2 large egg yolks

¼ cup [35 g] cornstarch

½ tsp kosher salt

½ cup [100 g] granulated sugar

2½ Tbsp unsalted butter

CORN-SHAPED BAO

1 recipe Basic Mantou (page 49)

½ tsp ground turmeric or 3 drops yellow food gel (optional)

½ tsp ceremonial-grade matcha or ½ drop green food gel (optional)

1 To make the corn custard, cut the **kernels** off the ears of corn (you should have 1⅔ cup [250 g]). Break the cobs in half, placing them in a medium pot along with the corn kernels and the **milk**. If you're using frozen or canned corn, skip the cobs and acknowledge it won't be as flavorful. Bring to a boil over medium-high heat, then lower the heat to medium-low and simmer for 5 minutes. Remove from the heat and allow it to steep for at least 1 hour.

2 Remove the cobs and strain the milk through a fine-mesh sieve, pressing on the kernels with the back of a spoon to get all the liquid out. Reserve the corn milk and 1 cup of the corn kernels and discard the rest.

3 In a medium mixing bowl, combine the **egg, egg yolks, cornstarch,** and **salt**. Whisk by hand until pale and fluffy, about 1 minute.

4 In a large mixing bowl, prepare an ice bath. It should be big enough for the egg mixture bowl to sit in.

5 In a medium pot, add the corn milk and stir in the **sugar**. Bring to a scald—small bubbles around the edges, right before boiling—over medium-high heat. Slowly pour the hot milk onto the egg mixture, whisking constantly to prevent the eggs from scrambling while they are tempered.

6 Return the mixture to the pot over medium-high heat and continue to whisk until it starts to boil and thicken, 3 to 5 minutes. Pour the custard back into the medium mixing bowl and give it another whisk to make sure everything is combined. Add the **butter** and emulsify using a stick blender (or a regular blender on low speed). Fold in the reserved corn kernels.

cont'd

7   Place a piece of plastic wrap against the surface of the custard to prevent a skin from forming. Place the bowl of custard over the ice bath to cool for 30 minutes, then refrigerate for 30 minutes more. If not using the same day, transfer to an airtight container and store for up to 3 days in the refrigerator.

8   To make the bao, make the **Basic Mantou** up to step 1.

9   If you are coloring your dough, divide the dough into quarters. Color three quarters of the dough yellow and one quarter of the dough green. Knead by hand until no streaks remain. (If you are not coloring your dough, skip this step.)

10   Lightly grease a medium mixing bowl with vegetable oil. Place the dough(s) into the bowl(s) and cover with plastic wrap. Allow the dough to proof until doubled in size, about 1 hour.

11   Punch the yellow dough down and turn it out onto a lightly floured work surface. Roll it into a log and portion it into seven equal [35 g] pieces. Take the green dough and portion it into seven equal [10 g] pieces. Cover with plastic wrap so they don't dry out. If you are not coloring your dough, divide the whole thing into seven equal [45 g] pieces.

12   Cut seven 4 in [10 cm] squares of parchment paper.

13   To shape like a corn, flatten a yellow piece of dough into a disc, then roll it out to a 3½ in [9 cm] circle. Take the straight edge of a bowl scraper or ruler and press grid lines into the dough, creating about ¼ in [6 mm] "kernels." Do not cut all the way through. Flip the dough over and place 2 Tbsp of the chilled corn custard in the center. Fold each side of the dough upward like a hard-shell taco and pinch the edges tightly to seal. It should now look like a dumpling.

Flip it over, seam-side down, and it should look like a corn cob! Take a piece of green dough and roll it into a log about ½ in [13 mm] thick. Roll the log out flat to a long oval, about 5 by 1 in [13 by 2.5 cm]. Grab your straight edge again and emboss several lines very close together lengthwise on the dough. Pinch it together in the middle and again at the ends, forming a point. It should look like a mustache now. Use your finger to dab a little water on the back of the green dough and wrap it around the bottom of the corn so it looks like the husk. Place it on a square of parchment and repeat with the rest. Proceed to step 15.

14   If shaping into round buns, flatten a piece of dough into a disc, then roll it out to a 3½ in [9 cm] circle. Place 2 Tbsp of the chilled corn custard in the center and gather the edges upward, pleating and pinching tightly to seal. Place it seam-side down on a square piece of parchment and repeat with the rest.

15 Place the bao on a baking sheet and cover loosely with plastic wrap. Allow the dough to proof until 50 percent larger, 45 minutes to 1 hour.

16 Prepare a two-basket steamer and bring the water to a boil. If you don't have two baskets, work in two batches. Place the bao in the baskets. Lower the heat to medium, cover, and steam for 10 minutes. Using oven mitts, carefully remove the steamer baskets from the water bath and set aside on a plate or tray. Keep covered and let them sit for 5 minutes before serving.

Pro Tips & Storage

- The bao are best served warm.

- Leftover bao can be stored in zip-top bags or airtight containers for up to 1 week in the refrigerator or 3 months in the freezer. Reheat in the microwave with a damp paper towel on top, or in the steamer.

- I highly recommend using fresh corn so you can use the cobs to add extra flavor while steeping, but if it's unavailable, frozen, thawed, or canned, drained, will work.

- The corn custard can be made in advance and stored in an airtight container for up to 4 days in the refrigerator.

Buckwheat & Black Sesame Bao

Steamed Buckwheat Bao with Sweet Black Sesame Filling

I never even thought about buckwheat until I had a galette complète in France: a savory buckwheat crêpe with Emmental cheese, ham, and an egg on top. The buckwheat flour brought crepes to a whole new level for me. It's toasty and nutty and crisps up in a different way than regular flour.

While in upstate New York for a girls' weekend, I was making buckwheat crêpe batter when I realized that buckwheat has a similar aroma to black sesame, that same kind of toasty-nuttiness. That's when the light bao-lb turned on—what if I made a steamed buckwheat bao and filled it with a more traditional black sesame filling? The result: a beautifully elegant harmony of flavors. I might even go so far as to say that buckwheat and black sesame should become a new classic flavor combination.

YIELD: Makes seven 1¾ oz [50 g] bao

BUCKWHEAT MANTOU

¾ cup + 1 Tbsp [100 g] cake flour

⅔ cup [100 g] buckwheat flour

¼ cup + 3 Tbsp [105 ml] whole milk

1 Tbsp granulated sugar

2 tsp vegetable oil

1 tsp instant yeast

¼ tsp kosher salt

BLACK SESAME FILLING

⅓ cup [45 g] toasted black sesame seeds

2½ Tbsp granulated sugar

2 Tbsp unsalted roasted peanuts

2 Tbsp unsalted butter, melted

1 Tbsp whole milk

Pinch kosher salt

1   To make the buckwheat mantou, in the bowl of a stand mixer fitted with the dough hook attachment, combine the cake flour, buckwheat flour, milk, sugar, oil, yeast, and salt. Knead on low speed until it comes together, about 1 minute, then increase to medium speed for 9 minutes more. The dough should look very smooth, like fondant.

2   Lightly grease a medium mixing bowl with vegetable oil. Turn the dough out into the bowl and cover with plastic wrap. Allow to proof until doubled in size, about 1 hour.

3   Meanwhile, make the black sesame filling. In the bowl of a food processor, combine the black sesame seeds, sugar, peanuts, butter, milk, and salt. Process until it turns into a paste, scraping down the bowl every now and then if necessary. Transfer to a bowl and cover with plastic wrap. Refrigerate until firm, about 30 minutes.

4   Scoop out 1 Tbsp of the filling and roll it into a ball. I use a cookie scoop, but if you don't have one, a spoon will work. Place it on a plate and repeat until you have seven balls of filling. Cover with plastic wrap and refrigerate until ready to use.

5   Punch down the dough and place it on a lightly floured work surface. Roll it into a log and portion it into seven equal [50 g] pieces. Cover

the pieces with plastic wrap so they don't dry out.

6   Cut seven 3 in [7.5 cm] squares of parchment paper.

7   Roll a piece of dough into a 12 in [30.5 cm] log. Cut it in half and place one piece on top of the other like a cross. Press the center of the cross down and place a ball of filling in the center. Pull one strand of dough over the filling, stretching it so it reaches the base of the other side, then another piece over that, weaving the other two pieces over and under like a lattice pie crust. Press the ends into the base of the bao and, if there are any open areas, pinch the dough together on the sides.

cont'd

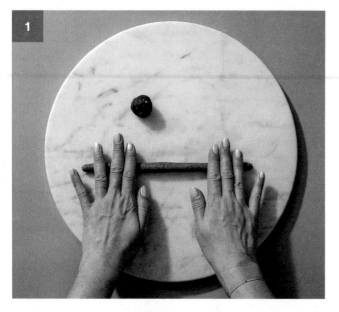

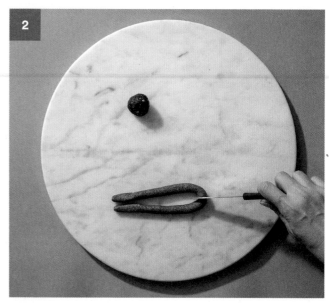

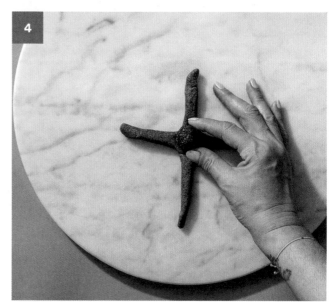

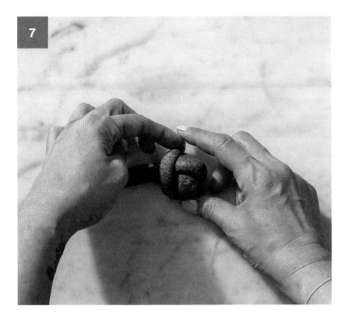

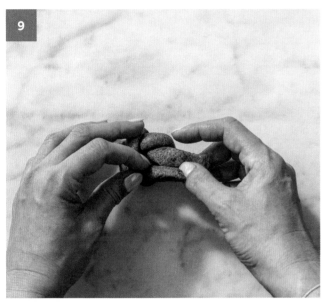

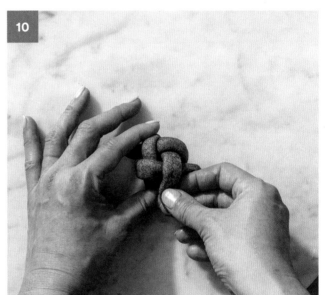

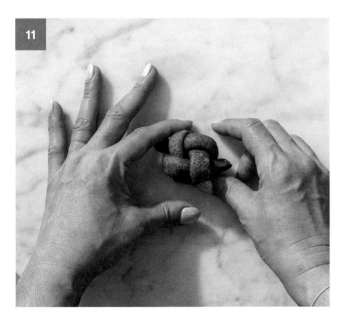

cont'd

BAO   CAKES & DESSERTS   SNACKS

8   Place the bao on a square of parch-
    ment and set aside on a 13 by 17 in
    [33 by 43 cm] baking sheet. Repeat
    with the others and cover the tray
    loosely with plastic wrap. Allow
    the buns to proof until 50 percent
    larger, about 45 minutes.

9   Prepare a two-basket steamer and
    bring the water to a boil. If you
    don't have two baskets, work in
    two batches. Place the bao in the
    baskets. Lower the heat to medium,
    cover, and steam for 10 minutes.
    Using oven mitts, carefully remove
    the steamer baskets from the water
    bath and set aside on a plate or tray.
    Keep covered and let them sit for
    5 minutes before serving.

Pro Tips & Storage

- The bao are best served warm.

- Leftover bao can be stored in zip-top
  bags or airtight containers for up to
  1 week in the refrigerator or 3 months
  in the freezer. Reheat in the microwave with a damp paper towel on
  top, or in the steamer.

- The filling can be made in advance
  and stored for up to 1 week in the
  refrigerator.

- Try swapping out the filling for
  Chinese Bacon, Egg & Chive Filling
  (page 57), Pastry Cream (page 117),
  Corn Custard (page 79), or Char Siu
  Carnitas (page 40).

Chestnut Bao

Steamed Chestnut-Shaped Chocolate Mantou with Chestnut Filling

My mom loves chestnuts. Every time we traveled to Hong Kong and saw a roasted chestnuts vendor, we had to stop and buy a bag. Then we saw them in Italy and France, and again, each time, we still had to buy a bag. Not much is cozier than a paper bag filled with freshly roasted chestnuts. I love how sweet and meaty they are and how they satisfy so many cravings at once.

In this recipe, I combined those memories and transformed them into these steamed chocolate bao filled with chestnut filling. The instructions describe how to make them into cute chestnut shapes, but if you can't be bothered with all that, they will be just as tasty if you shape them like regular bao.

YIELD: Makes ten 1¼ oz [35 g] bao

CHOCOLATE MANTOU

1 recipe Basic Mantou (page 49)

1½ Tbsp cocoa powder, preferably Dutch-process

1 Tbsp cake flour

CHESTNUT FILLING

1 cup [190 g] cooked chestnuts (packaged is fine if fresh are unavailable)

¾ cup [240 g] chestnut jam or paste

¼ tsp kosher salt

1   Make the **Basic Mantou** up to step 1, adding the **cocoa powder** with the rest of the ingredients.

2   If you want a regular bao shape, turn the dough into a medium mixing bowl lightly greased with vegetable oil, cover with plastic wrap, and allow to proof until doubled in size, about 1 hour. Proceed to step 4.

3   To shape like a chestnut, turn the dough out onto a lightly floured surface and divide it into four pieces. Take one piece and divide it in half, then take a half, add the **cake** flour, knead by hand until smooth; this will be the lighter color of the chestnut shape. Combine the rest of the pieces and knead by hand until smooth; this will be the darker color of the chestnut. Cover both colors of dough with plastic wrap and allow to proof until doubled in size, about 1 hour.

4   Meanwhile, make the chestnut filling. In the bowl of a stand mixer fitted with the paddle attachment, combine the **chestnuts**, **chestnut jam**, and **salt**. Cream together until fluffy and smooth, 2 to 3 minutes. Transfer to a bowl, cover with plastic wrap, and refrigerate until ready to use.

5   If you are making chestnut shapes, punch the darker dough down and place it on a lightly floured work surface. Roll it into a log and portion it into ten equal [30 g] pieces. Portion the lighter dough into ten equal [5 g] pieces. If you are not making chestnut shapes, divide the whole dough into ten equal [35 g]

pieces. Cover the dough pieces with plastic wrap so they don't dry out.

6   Cut ten 4 in [10 cm] squares of parchment paper.

7   Flatten a (darker) piece of dough into a disc, then roll it out to a 3½ in [9 cm] circle. Place 2 Tbsp of the chilled chestnut filling in the center and gather the edges of the dough upward, pleating and pinching to seal. Place it seam-side down on a square of parchment, and repeat with the rest. If making regular bao, proceed to step 9.

8   To shape them into chestnuts, take one bao and flatten slightly using the palm of your hand. Use your fingers to push a point at the top of the bao, forming it into a chestnut shape. Flatten a piece of the lighter dough. Use a rolling pin to roll it out into a thin oval shape. Dip your finger in a little water and dab it onto the dough. Pick it up and stick it to the bottom of the chestnut. Repeat with the rest.

cont'd

9 Place the bao on a baking sheet and cover loosely with plastic wrap. Allow to proof until 50 percent larger, about 45 minutes.

10 Prepare a two-basket steamer and bring the water to a boil. If you don't have two baskets, work in two batches. Place the bao in the baskets. Lower the heat to medium, cover, and steam for 10 minutes. Using oven mitts, carefully remove the steamer baskets from the water bath and set aside on a plate or tray. Keep covered and let them sit for 5 minutes before serving.

Pro Tips & Storage

- The bao are best served warm.

- Leftover bao can be stored in zip-top bags or airtight containers for up to 1 week in the refrigerator or 3 months in the freezer. Reheat in the microwave with a damp paper towel on top, or in the steamer.

- Try swapping the chestnut filling for Black Sesame Filling (page 82), Cherry Pie Filling (page 94), Strawberry-Rose Confit (page 101), Hojicha Milk Jam (page 101), Kaya Jam (page 107), Coconut Filling (page 109), Banana Jam (page 117), Pastry Cream (page 117), Ovaltine Ganache (page 174), Raspberry Ganache (page 188), Horlicks Ganache (page 192), or Marzipan (page 195).

Mantou Donuts

Mantou Donuts with Condensed Milk Glaze and Matcha

My mom used to make fried mantou, or Chinese steamed buns, as an after-school snack. They were like little fried pillows that you could dip into condensed milk for a surprisingly delicious bite. Unlike most fried treats, these bao are steamed before frying, creating a truly unique texture. The interior is bouncy and soft while the exterior has a toothsome chew. I never thought of them as donuts because real donuts are supposed to be circular with a hole in the middle, duh. Though it turns out, donuts can come in many different shapes and sizes. However, to make these instantly recognizable as donuts, I decided to shape mine into the more traditional American ring shape and coat them in a condensed milk glaze with a light dusting of matcha for a subtle savory finish.

YIELD: Makes eight 1½ oz [40 g] donuts

DONUTS

1 recipe Basic Mantou (page 49)

6 cups [1.4 L] vegetable oil

CONDENSED MILK GLAZE

3 cups [360 g] powdered sugar

6 Tbsp [90 g] unsalted butter, melted

¼ cup [76 g] sweetened condensed milk

2 Tbsp [30 ml] whole milk

¼ tsp kosher salt

1 Tbsp ceremonial-grade matcha (optional)

1   To make the donuts, make the Basic Mantou up to step 2.

2   Punch the dough down and place it on a lightly floured work surface. Roll it into a log and portion it into eight equal [40 g] pieces. Cover the pieces with plastic wrap so they don't dry out.

3   Cut eight 4 in [10 cm] squares of parchment paper.

4   On a lightly floured work surface, shape each piece of dough into a ball and then flatten slightly using the palm of your hand. Poke your finger in the center of the dough to create a hole. Place both your pointer fingers through the newly formed hole from the underside and gently pull apart while rotating to form a ring about 3 in [7.5 cm] diameter. It should now look like a donut. Repeat with the rest.

5   Place them on the parchment squares on a baking sheet and cover loosely with plastic wrap. Allow to proof until 50 percent larger, about 45 minutes.

6   Prepare a two-basket steamer and bring the water to a boil. If you don't have two baskets, work in two batches. Place the bao in the baskets. Lower the heat to medium, cover, and steam over a low simmer for 10 minutes. Using oven mitts, carefully remove the steamer baskets from the water bath and set aside on a plate or tray. Keep covered and let them sit for 5 minutes

before removing the lid. Allow the donuts to cool completely before frying.

7   In a large heavy-bottomed pot over high heat, bring the vegetable oil to 335°F [170°C].

8   Fry for 2 to 3 minutes on each side until golden brown, 5 to 6 minutes total.

9   Carefully remove the donuts using tongs or a spider and place on a paper towel–lined plate to cool completely.

10 Meanwhile, make the glaze. In a medium mixing bowl, whisk together the powdered sugar, butter, condensed milk, whole milk, and salt until smooth.

11 Completely submerge a donut into the glaze. Using two forks on either side of the donut, carefully lift it out of the glaze, scraping the bottom along the rim of the bowl to remove excess glaze. Place on a wire rack to set. Repeat with the rest.

cont'd

12 Once the glaze has set and is no longer sticky to the touch, use a fine-mesh sieve to lightly dust the tops with the matcha, if desired, and serve.

Pro Tips & Storage

- The donuts should be eaten the day of and are best served warm.

- The donuts can be steamed in advance and stored in zip-top bags or airtight containers for up to 3 days in the refrigerator or 3 months in the freezer. They need to be completely thawed and brought to room temperature before frying.

- Try substituting Vanilla Glaze (page 211), Chocolate Glaze (page 211), Hong Kong Milk Tea Glaze (page 209), or Coffee Glaze (page 209).

- Serve them alongside some Strawberry-Rose Confit (page 101), Hojicha Milk Jam (page 101), Kaya Jam (page 107), or Yuzu Curd (page 141).

Spiral Cherry Puffs
Deep-Fried Cherry Pie Puffs

One of my all-time favorite treats is the McDonald's seasonal cherry pie. I'm not talking about the kind you will find nowadays; I'm talking about the old school deep-fried kind. I have no idea why they swapped it out for a baked version, because the fried one was crispy and blistery perfection.

There is one technique of shaping sou that really allows the beauty of lamination to shine through flaky spirals on the exterior, like that of an Italian sfogliatella. I wanted to make my own version of the old-fashioned McDonald's cherry pie by shaping the sou like a Malaysian karipap, or curry puff, and filling it with a sweet and tangy cherry filling. It gets deep fried, then finished with a dusting of powdered sugar to accentuate the frilly layers.

YIELD: Makes 4 puffs

CHERRY PIE FILLING

3 cups [440 g] fresh or frozen red cherries, pitted

½ cup + 1 Tbsp [115 g] granulated sugar

2 Tbsp fresh lemon juice

¼ tsp kosher salt

2 Tbsp cornstarch

1 recipe Basic Sou (page 65)

6 cups [1.4 L] vegetable oil

Powdered sugar, for dusting (optional)

1 To make the cherry pie filling, in a medium saucepan, combine the **cherries, sugar, lemon juice,** and **salt.** Bring to a boil over medium-high heat, stirring occasionally. Lower the heat and simmer until the cherries have broken down and it looks syrupy, 15 minutes.

2 Make a slurry by whisking together 3 Tbsp of water and the **cornstarch.** Pour the mixture into the cherries while stirring and continue to sim-mer until thickened, about 2 min-utes more.

3 Remove from the heat and cool over an ice bath for 30 minutes before placing in the refrigerator to chill for at least 1 hour.

4 Make the **Basic Sou** up to step 2.

5 Place the water dough on a lightly floured surface and divide into four equal [60 g] pieces. Roll the oil dough into a log and portion it into four equal [30 g] pieces. Keep both doughs loosely covered with plastic wrap to prevent them from drying out.

6 Form the water dough pieces into balls, then roll the oil dough pieces into balls.

7 Take one piece of the water dough, flatten it with the palm of your hand, and roll it out to a 4 in [10 cm] disc. Place a ball of the oil dough in the center and wrap the water dough around it, pinching the seams to seal, creating a larger ball of dough. Repeat with the rest.

8 Take the first ball of dough you formed, flatten it with the palm of your hand, and roll it out to a long oval shape about 8 in [20 cm] long, 4 in [10 cm] wide, and ⅛ in [3 mm] thick. Roll it up lengthwise like a cinnamon roll. Repeat with the rest.

9 Take the first roll formed and with the spiraled side facing you, flatten it and roll it away from you into a rectangular shape about 2½ by 13 in [6 by 33 cm]. Roll it up lengthwise and repeat with the rest.

10 Take one roll and slice it in half; you should now have two spiral rolls. Lay one flat with the spiral side up and flatten it with the palm of your hand. Starting from the center of the spiral, roll it downward with a rolling pin. Rotate the spiral a little, and starting from the center, roll it downward. Keep rotating and rolling it out until you have a 5 in [13 cm] disc, about ⅛ in [3 mm] thick. It should be thin, but make sure there are no holes in the dough, or the filling will ooze out while frying.

cont'd

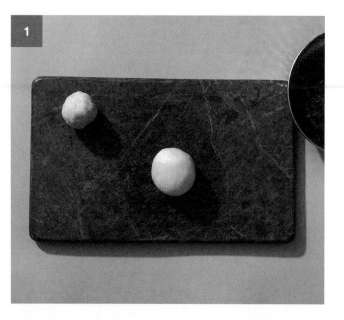

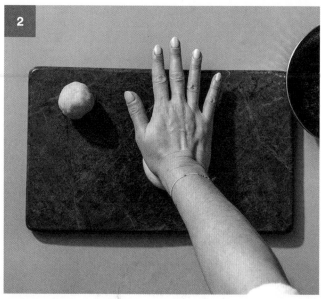

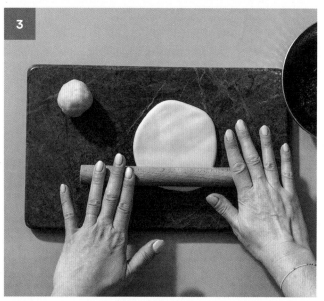

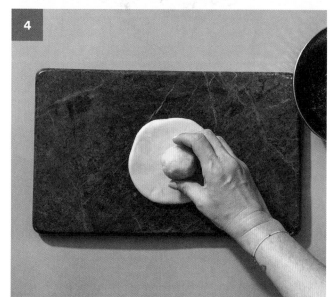

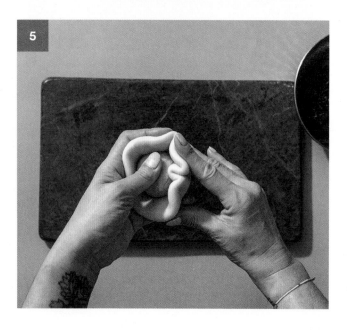

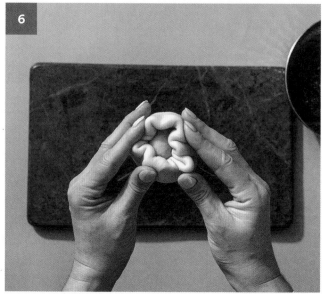

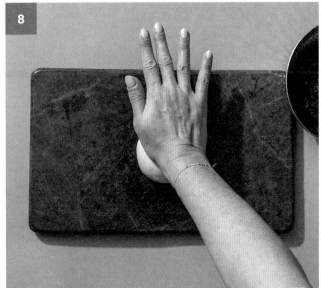

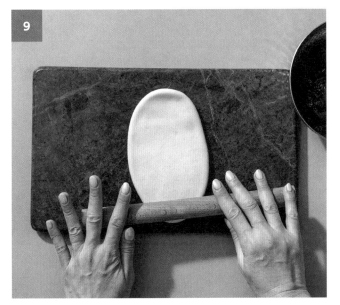

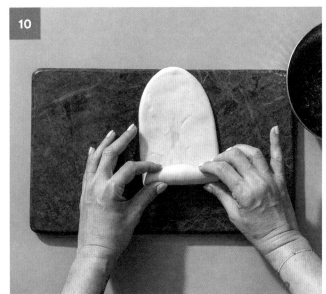

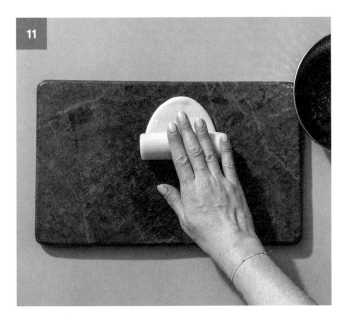

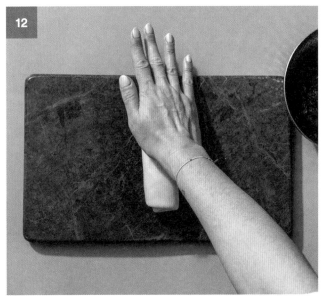

cont'd

BAO   CAKES & DESSERTS   SNACKS

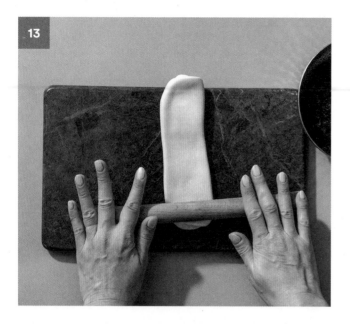

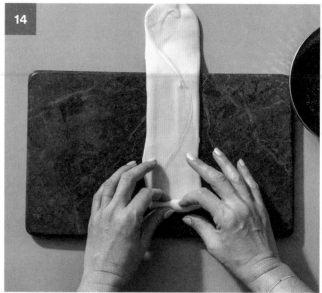

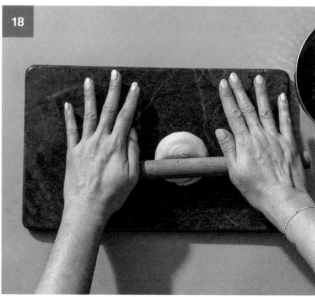

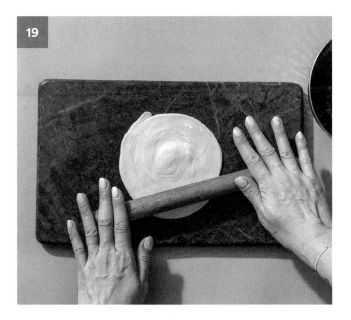

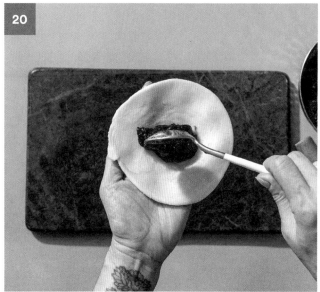

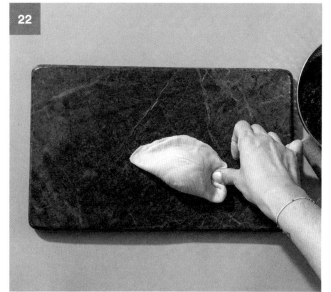

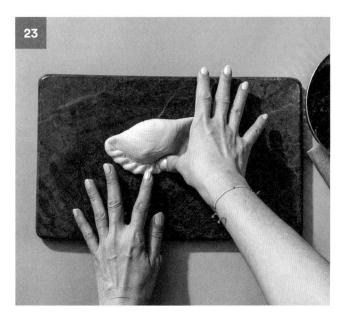

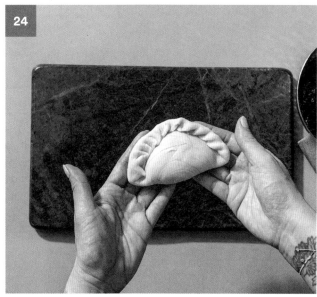

cont'd

11 Flip the disc over and place 2 Tbsp of the filling in the center. Fold it in half and pinch the edges together to seal. Starting from one side, fold the corner inward. Pull the corner of the new fold slightly and fold it over again like a pleat. Continue to go around the puff until the edge is completely pleated. Set aside and repeat with the rest.

12 In a large heavy-bottomed pot over high heat, bring the **vegetable oil** to 350°F [180°C]. Working in batches and without crowding the pot, fry a few puffs at a time, flipping them halfway through, until dark golden brown, 5 to 6 minutes total.

13 Using tongs or a spider, remove the puffs and transfer them to a paper towel–lined plate. Allow to cool completely before dusting with **powdered sugar**, if desired.

Pro Tips & Storage

- The puffs are best eaten the day of but can be kept in an airtight container for up to 2 days at room temperature.

- The dough can be made in advance and kept wrapped in plastic wrap for up to 3 days in the refrigerator or 3 months in the freezer.

- The rolling technique of starting in the center and rolling downward is a Chinese technique and the best way to accentuate the layers for the spiral puffs.

- Try filling the puffs with your favorite curry, Char Siu Carnitas (page 40), Dan Dan Filling (page 49), Hong Kong Bolognese (page 51), Kimchi–Corn Cheese Filling (page 55), Chinese Bacon, Egg & Chive Filling (page 57), Wild Mushroom–Boursin Filling (page 65), Black Sesame Filling (page 82), Chestnut Filling (page 87), or Coconut Filling (page 109).

Shokupan Donuts

As a kid, I was infatuated with Goober Grape, the Smucker's brand of peanut butter and jelly spread (who wasn't?). I was fascinated by its iconic tan and purple stripes and how they filled the jar that way. As an adult, I had a similar feeling of wonder when I discovered beautiful jars of Japanese layered milk and fruit jams. Japanese milk jam is made by cooking down milk, cream, and sugar until thickened. It is often flavored with tea and sometimes paired with a complementary fruit jam. Here I am pairing hojicha (roasted green tea) milk jam with strawberry-rose confit. Super light and fluffy shokupan donuts are the perfect vessel to highlight the deep roasted creaminess and delicate floral fruitiness of the jams.

YIELD: Makes 10 donuts

1 recipe Shokupan (page 35)

HOJICHA MILK JAM

2 cups [480 ml] whole milk

2 cups [480 ml] heavy cream

¼ cup [50 g] granulated sugar

¼ cup [35 g] whole milk powder

1 Tbsp hojicha tea powder

STRAWBERRY-ROSE CONFIT

1 lb [455 g] fresh strawberries, hulled and cut into ½ in [13 mm] chunks

1 cup [200 g] granulated sugar

¼ cup [60 ml] lemon juice, from about 2 lemons

½ tsp rose water

6 cups [1.4 L] vegetable oil

2 cups [400 g] granulated sugar

1 Make the shokupan up to step 4. While it's proofing, make the jams.

2 To make the hojicha milk jam, in a large heavy-bottomed pot, add the milk, cream, sugar, and milk powder. Whisk together and bring to a boil. Lower the heat to a simmer and continue to cook, stirring occasionally with a spatula and making sure to scrape the bottom of the pot, until reduced by half, 1 hour to 1 hour 15 minutes. It should be moderately bubbling the whole time.

3 Remove from the heat and whisk in the hojicha tea powder. Use a stick blender to emulsify until smooth, about 20 seconds. Strain the milk jam through a fine-mesh sieve into a mixing bowl and place it over an ice bath to cool.

4 To make the strawberry-rose confit, in a medium pot, combine the strawberries, sugar, and lemon juice. Bring to a boil over medium-high heat, then lower the heat to a simmer and continue to cook, stirring occasionally, until reduced by half and the temperature reaches 220°F [105°C], about 1 hour. It should be moderately bubbling the whole time. Transfer to a bowl and place it over an ice bath to cool.

5 Continuing with the shokupan, once it has doubled in size, punch it down and turn it out onto a lightly floured work surface. Roll the dough out to about ½ in [13 mm] thick.

6 Cut ten 4 in [10 cm] squares of parchment paper. Using a 2½ in [6 cm] circle cutter, stamp out rounds of dough, placing one on each piece of parchment. Cover loosely with plastic wrap or a tea towel and allow the donuts to proof until doubled in size again, 45 minutes to 1 hour.

cont'd

7 In a large heavy-bottomed pot over high heat, bring the **vegetable oil** to 350°F [180°C]. Carefully pick up one donut at a time by holding the corners of the parchment square and gently lower the whole thing into the oil, donut-side down.

8 After about 2 minutes the donuts will float to the top. Use tongs to gently peel off the parchment squares and discard. Fry until dark golden brown, 2 to 3 minutes on each side, 5 to 6 minutes total. Using tongs or a spider, remove the donuts from the oil and allow to cool on a wire rack or a paper towel–lined plate.

9 While the donuts are still slightly warm, roll them in the **sugar** to coat. Set them aside to cool completely.

10 Gather two piping bags and two round tips (Ateco 806). Prepare each bag with a piping tip, fill one with the milk jam, and the other with the strawberry-rose confit.

11 Use a chopstick to poke a hole on the side of each donut about two thirds of the way deep and gently slide it side to side, creating a pocket for the filling. Make sure not to poke the chopstick all the way through to the other side.

12 Fill each donut halfway with the milk jam. Fill the other half with the strawberry-rose confit, until the donut feels heavy and filling starts oozing out of the side.

Pro Tips & Storage

- The donuts should be eaten the day of.
- The jams can be kept in jars or airtight containers for up to 3 weeks in the refrigerator.
- If you can't find hojicha powder, you can substitute 4 tea bags or 1½ Tbsp of loose tea leaves. If you are using either of these options, follow step 2, and once the mixture has reduced by half, remove from the heat, blend it, then add the tea bags or leaves and let it steep for 20 minutes before straining through a fine-mesh sieve.
- Keep an eye on the oil temperature while frying. It is normal for the temp to dip once you put in the donuts, but if it doesn't rise back up you will need to regulate it. You want to keep it as close to 350°F [180°C] as possible.
- Try filling these donuts with Pastry Cream (page 117), Banana Jam (page 117), Matcha Cream (page 125), Mascarpone Cream (page 114), Yuzu Curd (page 141), Ube Cream (page 135), Royal Milk Tea Diplomat (page 204), Kaya Jam (page 107) or Kaya Cream (page 104).

Kaya French Toast

Kaya, meaning "rich" in Malay, is a coconut jam popular in all of Southeast Asia. Kaya toast is a popular Singaporean breakfast dish: a kaya jam sandwich on grilled white bread with a slab of cold butter in the center. It's typically served with a small dish of soft-boiled or poached eggs seasoned with dark soy and white pepper. The idea is to dip the sweet sandwich into the salty, jammy eggs and then wonder where this dish has been your whole life.

For my version, I am using a shokupan-base French toast, paired with a sweet, kaya-filled center, topped with soft whipped coconut kaya cream that oozes like lava when you cut into it. Living up to its name, it is deliciously rich without being overly sweet and makes for a perfect Sunday brunch dish.

YIELD: Makes 5 servings

1 recipe Shokupan (page 35)

ROYALE
4 large eggs
2 cups [480 ml] heavy cream
2 Tbsp granulated sugar
½ orange, zest only

KAYA CREAM
1 cup [240 ml] heavy cream
¼ cup [65 g] Kaya Jam (page 107)
¼ tsp kosher salt

½ cup [113 g] unsalted butter, at room temperature
Kaya Jam (page 107)
1 Tbsp ceremonial-grade matcha, for garnish (optional)

1 Make the **shokupan**. Follow the instructions for a Pullman loaf or regular loaf if you don't have a Pullman pan (step 7 or 8). Allow it to cool completely. It is actually better if the loaf is not fresh, so feel free to make it up to a week in advance if it suits your schedule.

2 To make the royale, in a blender, combine the **eggs, cream, sugar,** and **orange zest.** Process on low speed until smooth, about 15 seconds. Strain through a fine-mesh sieve into a shallow dish and set aside.

3 To make the kaya cream, in the bowl of a stand mixer fitted with the whisk attachment, whip together the **heavy cream, kaya jam,** and **salt** until it forms soft peaks. You want it loose enough so it flows slowly, like lava. Transfer to a bowl and cover with plastic wrap. Set aside in the refrigerator until ready to use.

4 Trimming off as little as possible, slice the crust off all the sides of the shokupan loaf. If you baked it in a regular loaf pan, trim the top off so the loaf looks like a rectangular box. Cut the loaf into five equal slices, each 1½ in [4 cm] thick.

5 Take one slice and cut it in half like you're making a sandwich. Each slice should now be ¾ in [2 cm] thick. Spread about ½ Tbsp of the **butter** on one side of each piece. Spread some plain **kaya jam** on top of the butter and sandwich both pieces of bread together with the jam in the center. Repeat with the rest of the slices.

6 Heat a large pan over medium heat and add the remaining 3 Tbsp of the butter. Dunk a sandwich into the royale, making sure to soak each side thoroughly, then place it in the pan and fry until nice and toasty, 2 to 3 minutes on each side. Add more butter to the pan if necessary for the rest.

cont'd

7   Place the French toast on a plate and, using the back of a spoon, push down on the top of the toast to make a shallow cavity. Fill the cavity with a large dollop of the kaya cream and garnish with a dusting of **matcha**, if desired. Serve immediately.

Pro Tips & Storage

- It's better to use bread that's a little old because it will be drier and able to soak up more of the royale. If you have the time, I suggest making the shokupan loaf 3 days to a week in advance.

- The kaya cream can be made in advance and stored for up to 3 days in the refrigerator.

- The royale can be made in advance and stored for up to 4 days in the refrigerator.

- Shokupan is a great bread for making French toast, so feel free to make it plain, too, without the kaya.

Kaya Jam

MAKES 2 CUPS

1 cup [240 ml] full-fat coconut milk

6 pandan leaves [30 g] or ¼ tsp pandan extract

½ cup [70 g] palm sugar or ¼ cup [50 g] light brown sugar + ¼ cup [50 g] granulated sugar

2 large eggs

3 large egg yolks

2 Tbsp granulated sugar

¼ tsp kosher salt

1 Pour the coconut milk into a blender and, using scissors, cut the pandan leaves into 1 in [2.5 cm] pieces into the coconut milk. Process until the leaves are the size of little specks. Let sit for 10 minutes. (If using pandan extract, skip this step and pour the coconut milk directly into a small pot. You will add the pandan extract in step 5.)

2 Using a fine-mesh sieve, strain the coconut milk mixture into a small pot. Use the back of a spoon to push all the liquid out of the pandan leaves. When you are left with nothing but pulp, gather it into a ball and squeeze it with your hand like you are squeezing out a wet sponge. Discard the pulp.

3 Chop or crumble the palm sugar and add it to a pot with the eggs, egg yolks, granulated sugar, and salt.

4 Whisk the mixture over medium-high heat until the sugar dissolves, then bring to a boil. Turn the heat down to keep it at a simmer (it should be slowly bubbling the whole time) until thickened and curdled, 5 to 10 minutes more. It will look broken, but don't worry, we will fix it in the next step.

5 Strain the jam through a fine-mesh sieve into a mixing bowl or blender jar. (If you are using pandan extract, add it here.) Use a stick blender (or a regular blender on low speed) to blend until emulsified and smooth, about 30 seconds.

6 Transfer to an airtight container or jar and refrigerate until chilled, about 2 hours.

Pro Tips & Storage

- The kaya jam can be made in advance and stored for up to 2 weeks in the refrigerator.

- I highly recommend using fresh pandan leaves. If they are unavailable and you use pandan extract, note that the color will be much brighter.

Mama Lam's Coconut Croissants
Chinese Coconut Cocktail Buns

Who remembers replying "chicken butt" when asked "what's up?" as a kid? That always made me think of my mom's gai mei bao, or "chicken butt buns" in Cantonese. These bao are made with a delicious buttery coconut filling, and my sister and I always wanted to help her make them. My mom shaped each one uniformly and identically to the next without even using a scale, all lined up like little bao soldiers ready to be eaten, while my sister and I created the most ridiculous shapes like ravioli, triangles, and worms. As an ode to my constant shapeshifting, both in baking and in life, I have taken my mom's recipe and formed them into gorgeous croissants, perfect for breakfast.

YIELD: Makes 12 croissants

1 recipe Shokupan (page 35)

COCONUT FILLING

2 cups [200 g] sweetened coconut flakes

½ cup [100 g] granulated sugar

6 Tbsp [90 g] unsalted butter, melted

¼ tsp kosher salt

1 recipe Egg Wash (page 35)

1   Make the **shokupan** up to step 5. Line a 13 by 17 in [33 by 43 cm] baking sheet with parchment paper.

2   To make the coconut filling, in a food processor, combine the **coconut flakes, sugar, butter,** and **salt.** Pulse until everything comes together and the flakes look more like confetti, about 20 seconds.

3   Roll out the bread dough into a rectangle, about 7 by 13 in [18 by 33 cm]. Sprinkle the coconut mixture all over the dough and gently spread and press using your fingertips. Fold the rectangle in half crosswise and press the edges to seal. The rectangle should now be closer to square in shape. Place it onto the prepared baking sheet and chill in the refrigerator for 15 minutes.

4   Dust a work surface with all-purpose flour and roll out the dough once more, about 12 by 22 in [30 by 56 cm] and about ¼ in [3 to 6 mm] thick. Trim off as little as you can on the longer sides to make straight edges.

5   Using a ruler and paring knife, mark little notches 1½ in [4 cm] apart at the base of the longer side of the rectangle. On every other notch, use the edge of the ruler to lightly mark a perpendicular line. Then use the edge of the ruler to lightly mark a diagonal line connecting the first notch to the top of the perpendicular line. Mark again from that point to the third notch. You should have marked out an isosceles triangle with a line running vertically through the center. Continue to mark out triangles on the rest of the dough.

6   Cut out the triangles; you should have about twelve pieces. Fold the corners of the base inward to meet one another at the midpoint. Then lightly fold that tab over and roll it up. Place the croissant on the prepared baking sheet and repeat with the rest. Cover loosely with plastic wrap and allow to proof until doubled in size, about 1 hour.

cont'd

7 Preheat the oven to 375°F [190°C]. Brush the tops of each croissant with two coats of **egg wash** and bake until deep golden brown, 25 to 30 minutes. Allow the croissants to cool on the baking sheet or wire rack.

Pro Tips & Storage

- The croissants can be kept in zip-top bags for up to 3 days at room temperature, 1 week in the refrigerator, or 3 months in the freezer. Just make sure to warm them before consuming.

- The filling can be made and stored in an airtight container or flattened into a disc and double-wrapped in plastic wrap for up to 1 week in the refrigerator or up to 3 months in the freezer. Thaw completely at room temperature before using.

- Enjoy a croissant with a cup of hot milk tea or coffee for a delicious breakfast or afternoon snack.

Vietnamese Cinnamon-Raisin Babka

Shokupan Loaf Swirled with Brown Sugar, Cinnamon & Raisins

Pepperidge Farm cinnamon raisin bread was a pantry staple in the Lam household. A simple slice of it toasted with butter, and somehow, it was the best thing I ever tasted. This recipe is that memory one hundred times over. I use Vietnamese cinnamon (also known as Saigon cinnamon), which has a much more intense flavor than regular cinnamon, swirled with caramelized sticky brown sugar and plump raisins. Part cinnamon roll and part loaf, it gets shaped in the same style as a beautiful babka for a bold flavor with every bite.

YIELD: Makes 1 loaf

1 recipe Shokupan (page 35)

CINNAMON SWIRL

1 cup [200 g] dark brown sugar

4 Tbsp [55 g] unsalted butter, melted

1 Tbsp ground Vietnamese cinnamon or regular cinnamon

½ tsp kosher salt

½ cup [70 g] raisins (optional)

STREUSEL

3 Tbsp dark brown sugar

2 Tbsp unsalted butter, at room temperature

¼ cup [30 g] almond flour

3 Tbsp all-purpose flour

½ tsp kosher salt

¼ tsp ground Vietnamese cinnamon or regular cinnamon

1 recipe Egg Wash (page 35)

1 Make the shokupan up to step 5.

2 To make the cinnamon swirl, in a small mixing bowl, combine the brown sugar, butter, cinnamon, and salt. Stir to combine.

3 Roll the dough out into a 10 by 12 in [25 by 30.5 cm] rectangle. Sprinkle the cinnamon filling all over the dough, gently spreading and pressing it down with your fingertips. Sprinkle the raisins, if using, on top.

4 With the long side of the dough facing you, roll it up into a log, pinching the seam to seal. Wrap the log in a piece of parchment paper and refrigerate for 15 minutes. Grease an 8½ by 4½ in [21.5 by 11 cm] loaf pan with nonstick spray or butter.

5 Place the dough log on a cutting board, flatten it slightly with the palm of your hand, and cut it in half vertically, exposing the inside.

6 Twist the two pieces together and place into the prepared loaf pan. Cover with a tea towel and let proof until doubled in size, about 1 hour.

7 Meanwhile, make the streusel. In the bowl of a stand mixer fitted with the paddle attachment, cream together the brown sugar and butter until light and fluffy, about 1 minute.

8 Scrape down the sides and bottom of the bowl and add the almond flour, all-purpose flour, salt, and cinnamon. Mix on medium speed until it forms crumbles the size of little pebbles. Transfer the streusel to a parchment-lined dish in a flat layer and place in the freezer until ready to use.

cont'd

9 Preheat the oven to 375°F [190°C]. Brush the top of the babka with two coats of **egg wash** and sprinkle the streusel all over the top. Bake until dark golden brown and the internal temperature measures 200°F [95°C], 35 to 40 minutes. Allow to cool completely in the pan before slicing and serving.

Pro Tips & Storage

- The babka can be kept in a zip-top bag or double plastic wrapped for up to 4 days at room temperature, 1 week in the refrigerator, or 3 months in the freezer. Just make sure to toast or warm it before consuming.

- Cut the loaf into thinner slices for toast and top it with butter and salt, or try drizzling it with some sweetened condensed milk.

- Cut thicker slices and use it to make Kaya French Toast (page 104).

- Turn it into cinnamon rolls by slicing the log into 1½ in [4 cm] segments (instead of twisting) and baking them in an 8 or 9 in [20 or 23 cm] greased skillet or square or round pan for 30 to 35 minutes.

Strawberry-Mascarpone Maritozzi

Shokupan Cream Buns

You can find milk bread cream buns in almost every Asian bakery. They usually come round or elongated, slit across the top, and filled with piped swirls of whipped cream in varying flavors. This is one of those foods that, to nobody's surprise, has traveled far and wide and made it as a staple bakery item in many different countries around the world. Italy has its own version called a maritozzo.

For my rendition, I use shokupan as the base and fill it with strawberry-rose confit, orange-scented mascarpone cream, and fresh strawberries. Then I top the whole thing off with a strawberry shortcake crunch reminiscent of the nostalgic ice cream truck classic. The result is a heavenly fresh sweet treat that pairs perfectly with a cup of milk tea.

YIELD: Makes 10 buns

---

1 recipe Shokupan (page 35)

½ recipe Strawberry-Rose Confit (page 101)

STRAWBERRY SHORTCAKE CRUNCH

½ recipe Bolo Topping (page 40)

1 cup [22 g] freeze-dried strawberries

1 Tbsp powdered sugar

1 Tbsp unsalted butter, melted

¼ tsp kosher salt

MASCARPONE CREAM

1 cup [240 g] mascarpone

½ cup [60 g] powdered sugar

½ vanilla bean, seeds scraped, or 1 tsp vanilla extract

1 orange, zest only

1½ cups [360 ml] heavy cream

¼ tsp kosher salt

GARNISH

20 fresh medium-sized strawberries, hulled

2 Tbsp powdered sugar

1   Make the **shokupan** up to step 6, but portion the dough into ten equal [60 g] pieces. Then continue with the rest of the recipe through step 11. Set the buns aside to cool completely.

2   Make the **strawberry-rose confit** and **bolo topping** steps 8 through 11.

3   To make the strawberry shortcake crunch, preheat the oven to 350°F [180°C]. Peel the top parchment off the rolled bolo topping and place the whole sheet onto a 13 by 17 in [33 by 43 cm] baking sheet. Bake until golden brown, about 12 minutes. Remove from the oven and let cool on the baking sheet.

4   Take about three quarters of the baked bolo topping [200 g] (eat the rest), break it up into smaller pieces, and place in a food processor. Pulse several times until the pieces are about the same size as the freeze-dried strawberries.

5   Add the **freeze-dried strawberries, powdered sugar, butter,** and **salt** to the food processor. Pulse again until you have a crumble the size of lentils. Set aside in a shallow dish.

6   To make the mascarpone cream, in the bowl of a stand mixer fitted with the whisk attachment, combine the **mascarpone, powdered sugar, vanilla,** and **orange zest** and whisk on medium speed to combine, about 30 seconds.

7   Scrape down the sides of the bowl and, with the machine running on medium-low, drizzle in the **heavy cream.** Then add the **salt.** Continue to whisk on medium-high speed until stiff peaks form. Do not overwhip.

8   Take a bun and slice the top down the center; do not cut all the way through. Open up the bun like a clam shell and spread a thin layer of the confit on both sides of the interior of the bun, then add 1 Tbsp of confit on the bottom.

cont'd

9 Place a larger **strawberry** point-side down in the middle of the bun, on top of the confit. Using a spoon or offset spatula, fill the bun with mascarpone cream and smooth it out on the top so it's flush with the bun edges.

10 Carefully pick up a maritozzo and dunk the cream center into the strawberry shortcake crunch. Use a fine-mesh sieve to lightly dust the top of the bun with **powdered sugar**. Garnish with a smaller strawberry, if desired. Repeat steps 8, 9, and 10 with the rest.

Pro Tips & Storage

- Completed maritozzi can be kept in airtight containers for up to 3 days in the refrigerator. I do not recommend freezing.

- The bao alone can be premade and kept in zip-top bags or airtight containers for up to 4 days at room temperature, 1 week in the refrigerator, or 3 months in the freezer.

- The strawberry shortcake crunch can be made in advance and stored in an airtight container (preferably with a desiccant pack) for up to 3 days at room temperature or 1 week in the refrigerator.

- The mascarpone cream can be made in advance and kept in an airtight container for up to 4 days in the refrigerator.

- If you don't like mascarpone, you can substitute cream cheese, or just fill with a plain or Stabilized Malted Chantilly (page 175).

- Feeling lazy? You can substitute store-bought jam and crushed vanilla wafers or vanilla Oreos.

Chocolate-Banana Bolo Bao
Chocolate Bolo Bao Filled with Banana Custard

Bolo bao is a staple in every Chinese bakery and also happens to be one of my personal favorites. Meaning "pineapple bun" in Chinese, this soft, pillowy bun is topped with a crackly cookie top, similar to the Japanese melon pan or the Mexican concha. Though named after one of my favorite fruits, there is actually zero pineapple involved in the process here. Its name refers to its signature golden-hued topping that resembles the spiky rind of a pineapple. Here, I have turned the traditional sweet bao into a chocolate version filled with yet another favorite American dessert of mine, banana pudding. It's a match made in heaven.

YIELD: Makes 12 buns

TANG ZHONG

¼ cup [60 ml] whole milk

¼ cup [60 ml] cold water

3 Tbsp bread flour

CHOCOLATE BOLO BAO DOUGH

1¾ cups [265 g] bread flour

⅓ cup [90 g] tang zhong

¼ cup [50 g] granulated sugar

3 Tbsp heavy cream

2 Tbsp whole milk

2 large eggs

3 Tbsp Dutch-process cocoa powder

2 tsp instant yeast

1½ tsp whole milk powder

1 tsp kosher salt

2 Tbsp unsalted butter, at room temperature and cubed

PASTRY CREAM

1 large egg

2 large egg yolks

¼ cup [40 g] cornstarch

2 tsp vanilla extract

½ tsp kosher salt

2 cups [480 ml] whole milk

½ cup [100 g] granulated sugar

BANANA JAM

3 large bananas, peeled and diced into ½ in [13 mm] cubes

½ cup + 2 Tbsp [130 g] granulated sugar

1 Tbsp dark brown sugar

1 large lemon, juice only

1 tsp vanilla extract

¼ tsp kosher salt

CRACKLY TOP

1 cup [200 g] granulated sugar

½ cup [113 g] unsalted butter, cubed, at room temperature

2 large eggs, yolks only (save the whites for the egg wash)

2 tsp vanilla extract

1 cup + 2 Tbsp [170 g] all-purpose flour

2 Tbsp + 1 tsp Dutch-process cocoa powder

½ tsp kosher salt

½ tsp baking powder

EGG WASH

2 large egg whites, reserved from the crackly top recipe

1 To make the tang zhong, in a small pot, combine the milk, cold water, and flour. Bring to a boil, whisking, over medium-high heat and continue whisking until it turns into a thick paste, 3 to 5 minutes. Remove from the heat and transfer the tang zhong to a small bowl to let cool to room temperature.

2 To make the dough, in the bowl of a stand mixer fitted with the dough hook attachment, add the flour, ⅓ cup of tang zhong (discard the rest), the sugar, cream, milk, eggs, cocoa powder, yeast, milk powder, and salt. Mix on low speed until well combined, 3 minutes, then mix on medium speed until smooth and elastic, an additional 7 minutes.

3 With the machine running, add the butter a couple of cubes at a time, allowing the dough to come back together before adding more. Once all the butter has been added, continue to mix on medium speed until the butter is fully incorporated and

cont'd

you can pull a window, 2 minutes more. The dough will be sticky.

4   Grease a large bowl with nonstick spray, butter, or vegetable oil. Turn the dough out into the bowl and cover with a tea towel. Let it proof until doubled in size, 1 hour 30 minutes to 2 hours.

5   Meanwhile, make the pastry cream. In a large mixing bowl, prepare an ice bath. In a medium mixing bowl, combine the **egg, egg yolks, cornstarch, vanilla,** and **salt**. Whisk by hand until pale and fluffy, about 1 minute.

6   In a medium saucepan, combine the **milk** and **sugar**. Bring to a scald—small bubbles around the edges, right before boiling—over medium-high heat. Slowly pour the hot milk into the eggs, whisking constantly to prevent the eggs from scrambling.

7   Return the egg mixture to the pot and continue to whisk over medium-high heat until it starts to boil and thicken, 3 to 5 minutes. Transfer the pastry cream to a bowl and place a piece of plastic wrap directly touching the surface to prevent a skin from forming. Place over the ice bath to cool for 30 minutes, then refrigerate for at least 30 minutes more.

8   To make the banana jam, in a small pot, combine the **bananas, granulated sugar, brown sugar, lemon juice,** 1 Tbsp of water, the **vanilla,** and **salt.**

9   Place over medium-high heat, stirring occasionally, until it boils. Lower the heat to medium-low and simmer until the bananas are caramelized and jammy, about 12 minutes.

10 Transfer the jam to another bowl to cool. Let it sit at room temperature for at least 45 minutes.

11 Line two 13 by 17 in [33 by 43 cm] baking sheets with parchment paper. Punch down the dough and turn it out onto a lightly floured work surface. Portion the dough into twelve equal [50 g] pieces. To shape the buns, take one portion of the dough and flatten it using the palm of your hand. Fold all the edges inward and pinch it shut; it should kind of look like a dumpling. Turn the ball of dough seam-side down onto your work surface and cup your hand over it between the edge of your hand and the fleshy part under your thumb. Roll in a circular motion, trying to keep the seam constantly on the surface, until it forms a tight ball. Repeat with the rest, placing six buns on each baking sheet. Cover each sheet loosely with plastic wrap and let the buns proof again until doubled in size, about 1 hour.

12 Meanwhile, make the crackly tops. In the bowl of a stand mixer fitted with the paddle attachment, combine the **sugar** and **butter**. Mix on medium speed until light and fluffy, about 2 minutes. Scrape down the sides of the bowl, add one **egg yolk,** mix until just combined. Then

cont'd

add the second yolk and the vanilla and mix until fully combined.

13 Scrape down the sides of the bowl and add the flour, cocoa powder, salt, and baking powder. Turn the mixer back on, starting at a low speed to avoid it exploding in your face. Once everything has settled, turn it up to medium speed and continue to mix until everything is completely incorporated, about 1 minute. It should resemble cookie dough.

14 Divide the dough in half and place one portion in between two pieces of parchment paper roughly measuring 12 by 16 in [30.5 by 40.5 cm]. Roll it out to ⅛ in [3 mm] thick, mimicking the shape of the parchment. Place on a baking sheet and put it in the refrigerator to chill for 15 minutes. Repeat with the other portion of dough.

15 Preheat the oven to 375°F [190°C]. Make an egg wash by whisking together the reserved egg whites and ½ tsp of water.

16 Working with one baking sheet at a time, peel off one side of parchment, gently lay it back on the dough, flip, and peel off the other side. Use a 3½ in [9 cm] circle cookie cutter to cut out twelve discs. Save the scraps and reroll them again between two sheets of parchment paper to cut more discs.

17 Using a pastry brush, gently brush a coat of egg wash on top of each bun. Lightly place one cookie disc on top of each bun and gently press it to stick. Brush the tops of the cookies with more egg wash. Bake until the tops are cracked and set and the bottoms of the buns are darker brown, 15 to 18 minutes. Cool completely on the baking sheets or wire racks.

18 Stir the cooled pastry cream until smooth and fold in the banana jam until completely incorporated. Transfer to a pastry bag fitted with a ⅜ in [9.5 mm] round piping tip (Ateco 804).

19 Use a chopstick to poke holes in the bottom of each bun. I like to insert the chopstick at an angle parallel to the base and swivel the chopstick around to create some space in the center of the bao for the filling. If you don't have a chopstick, you can use a metal straw or paring knife. Be careful not to poke it through the bread or too close to the edges.

20 Holding a bun hole-side up in the palm of your hand, pipe the custard into each bao until it feels heavy and begins to overflow. Scrape off any excess and repeat with the remaining buns.

Pro Tips & Storage

- Baked, unfilled bolo bao can be kept in zip-top bags for up to 1 day at room temperature, 1 week in the refrigerator, or 3 months in the freezer.

- Filled bao can be kept in zip-top bags for up to 4 days in the refrigerator or 3 months in the freezer.

- If you have extra crackly cookie dough, you can save it for the next time, wrapped or rolled between parchment for 1 week in the refrigerator or 3 months in the freezer. The dough can only be rerolled once.

- Pastry cream can be kept in an airtight container for up to 4 days in the refrigerator. I do not recommend freezing it. This is a great basic pastry cream recipe that can be used for tarts, cakes, fillings, and more. Make sure to paddle it until smooth before using.

- The banana jam can be kept in an airtight container for up to 2 weeks in the refrigerator. Enjoy it on toast or in any other jam application.

- Try swapping out the banana jam with the Coconut Filling from Mama Lam's Coconut Croissants (page 109). To do this, fill the bao before baking using the same shaping method as Char Siu Carnitas Bolo Bao (page 40), and bake as directed.

- Try filling them with just the pastry cream, just the banana jam, Matcha Cream (page 125), Strawberry-Rose Confit (page 101), or Hojicha Milk Jam (page 101).

CAKES & DESSERTS

Also known as the pastry chef section, this chapter focuses on large-format cakes and show-stopping desserts. Here, you will learn how multiple components are pieced together to form one cohesive dish that is worthy enough to serve in any restaurant or bakery, or in the comfort of your home.

Drawing inspiration from desserts across the globe, I pair my best food memories with some of my favorite Asian ingredients and flavors in a way that makes sense and will make you question how this wasn't its original presentation.

By using Asian, American, French, and Latin baking techniques, you will cross borders and bridge gaps to create spectacular sweets from cakes to tarts, custards to mille feuille, and no-churn ice creams to jellies.

Matcha-Azuki Mont Blanc

One of my favorite Parisian chestnut desserts is a mont blanc, or "white mountain," named after the highest peak in the Alps. This dessert is domed with swirled strands of chestnut purée and a dusting of powdered sugar mimicking the snow-capped mountain. For my version, I use a matcha sablé base filled with a crunchy meringue dome and matcha whipped cream, topped with oodles of noodle-like strands of azuki, a Japanese red bean paste. It may be hard for some people to get past the idea of eating beans for dessert, but trust me, it tastes nothing like a bean; it is in fact very similar to a chestnut purée. It has a sweet, mildly earthy, and nutty flavor that pairs well with matcha, contrasts perfectly with the airy meringue, and balances out the fluffy cream.

YIELD: Makes one 8 in [20 cm] tart

MERINGUE

3 large egg whites

¼ tsp kosher salt

¾ cup [90 g] powdered sugar

¼ cup + 3 Tbsp [95 g] granulated sugar

MATCHA SABLÉ

5 Tbsp [70 g] unsalted butter, at room temperature

⅓ cup [40 g] powdered sugar

1 large egg yolk

1 cup [125 g] cake flour, sifted

1½ tsp ceremonial-grade matcha

¼ tsp kosher salt

MATCHA CREAM

1 cup [240 ml] heavy cream

¼ cup [30 g] powdered sugar

1 tsp ceremonial-grade matcha

¼ tsp kosher salt

17 oz [500 ml] can sweetened red bean paste

1 Tbsp powdered sugar (optional)

1 Preheat the oven to 250°F [120°C]. Trace a 6 in [15 cm] circle on a sheet of parchment paper, flip it over, and place it on a baking sheet.

2 To make the meringue, in the bowl of a stand mixer fitted with the whisk attachment, whip the egg whites and salt on medium speed until frothy, about 30 seconds.

3 In a small mixing bowl, whisk together the powdered sugar and granulated sugar until there are no lumps. With the mixer running, stream about one third of the sugar into the egg whites in three additions, with about 30 seconds in between each addition. Continue mixing until stiff peaks form, 3 to 5 minutes.

4 Transfer the meringue to the center of the traced circle on the prepared parchment. Use a small offset spatula or back of a spoon to smooth it out into a dome shape. Color inside the lines! Make sure to stay within the circle, as it will increase when it

bakes and it needs to fit inside the tart shell.

5 Bake until cooked through but still pale, 1 hour 30 minutes. Remove from the oven and allow to cool at room temperature.

6 Meanwhile, make the matcha sablé. In the bowl of a stand mixer fitted with the paddle attachment, cream together the butter and powdered sugar until light and fluffy, 2 to 3 minutes.

7 Add the egg yolk and mix to combine. Scrape down the sides of the bowl and add the cake flour, matcha, and salt. Mix until the dough just comes together.

8 Gather the dough into a disc, wrap in plastic wrap, and place in the refrigerator to chill for 30 minutes.

9 Roll out the dough on a lightly floured surface and gently transfer it to an 8 in [20 cm] tart pan. Lay it loosely in the center of the pan and, without stretching or pulling the

cont'd

dough, press it into the corners and up the sides. Trim off any excess with a small paring knife or run your rolling pin over the top to cut it. Place the tart shell in the refrigerator to chill for at least 15 minutes while you preheat the oven to 350°F [180°C].

10 Prick all over the bottom of the tart shell with a fork and blind bake the shell until lightly browned around the edges, 12 to 15 minutes. If the dough has puffed up when you take it out of the oven, use the back of a spoon to press it back flat. Allow it to cool completely before unmolding.

11 To make the matcha cream, in the bowl of a stand mixer fitted with the whisk attachment, whip the **cream, powdered sugar, matcha,** and **salt** until stiff peaks form.

12 Spread a ¼ in [6 mm] thick layer of matcha cream in the bottom of the tart shell. Place the meringue dome on top, then scoop the rest of the matcha cream on top of the dome. Using an offset spatula or the back of a spoon, spread it around the meringue dome to form a mountain shape. Place it in the refrigerator for 15 minutes.

13 In the bowl of a stand mixer fitted with the paddle attachment, cream the **red bean paste** until smooth, about 1 minute. Transfer the paste to a piping bag fitted with a large hair/grass/mont blanc piping tip (I use JEM 235).

14 Pipe the azuki paste over the mountain of matcha cream in a circular motion, starting from the bottom and going around and around until you reach the top. It should look like a big pile of noodles. Dust the top with **powdered sugar,** if desired.

Pro Tips & Storage

- Any leftovers can be stored in an airtight container for up to 3 days in the refrigerator.

- The matcha sablé can be made up to 3 days in advance and kept wrapped in plastic wrap in the refrigerator.

- I highly recommend using ceremonial-grade matcha if accessible. That's what's gonna give you the bright green color versus muddy swamp. It's expensive, but for me, worth it.

Pandan-Lime Meringue Pie

Once upon a time, I participated in a baking competition television series whose premise involved recreating iconic American desserts from around the country. For one of the challenges, the theme was Florida, and I made my take on a key lime pie, which was not exactly this recipe, but I did make the same exact pandan-lime curd as below and instead put it on top of a pavlova shell. It ultimately saved my behind and kept me in the competition long enough to make it to the semifinals.

This dessert feels like a coconut shell garnished with a paper umbrella under a thatched roof on a beautiful island in the Philippines.

YIELD: Makes one 9 in [23 cm] pie

PANDAN-LIME CURD

¾ tsp gelatin powder (optional, see Pro Tips)

⅔ cup [130 g] granulated sugar

½ cup + 1 Tbsp [135 ml] fresh lime juice

3 large eggs

½ tsp pandan extract

¼ tsp kosher salt

½ cup + 3 Tbsp [160 g] unsalted butter, cubed, cold

RITZ CRACKER CRUST

1½ sleeves [48 pieces or 150 g] Ritz crackers

½ cup [113 g] unsalted butter, melted

½ cup [50 g] sweetened coconut flakes

3 Tbsp palm sugar or light or dark brown sugar

½ tsp kosher salt

SWISS MERINGUE

3 large egg whites

⅔ cup [130 g] granulated sugar

¼ tsp kosher salt

1 To make the pandan-lime curd, in a small dish, add 1 Tbsp of water and sprinkle over the gelatin, if using. Quickly stir to combine and set aside to bloom.

2 In a small pot, whisk together the sugar, lime juice, and eggs. Cook over medium-high heat, whisking continuously, until thickened, about 13 minutes. Remove from the heat and add the bloomed gelatin. Whisk until completely dissolved.

3 Strain the curd through a fine-mesh sieve over a bowl to remove any egg or gelatin bits. Add the pandan extract, salt, and cubed butter. Whisk until the extract is fully incorporated, then use a stick blender (or a regular blender on low speed) to emulsify the butter until silky smooth.

4 Place a piece of plastic wrap directly on the surface of the curd to prevent a skin from forming. Place the bowl over an ice bath to cool for 30 minutes.

5 Meanwhile, make the Ritz crust. Preheat the oven to 350°F [180°C]. In the bowl of a food processor, combine the Ritz crackers, melted butter, coconut flakes, palm sugar, and salt. Process until it looks like coarse, wet sand.

6 Press the crumbs into a 9 in [23 cm] pie dish, dispersing them evenly on the bottom and up the sides. Bake until golden brown on the edges, 12 minutes. Remove from the oven and let cool completely.

7 Remove the curd from the ice bath and stir until smooth. Pour the curd into the cooled pie shell, smooth out the top, and refrigerate until set, at least 2 hours.

cont'd

8 To make the Swiss meringue, in a medium pot, bring about 2 in [5 cm] of water to a boil over high heat. The pot should be big enough to hold the bowl of a stand mixer on the rim without touching the water. Place the **egg whites, sugar,** and **salt** in the bowl of the stand mixer. Place it over the pot and whisk continuously until it reaches 160°F [70°C], about 5 minutes. This is to cook out any bacteria that may be in the raw eggs.

9 Place the bowl in the stand mixer fitted with the whisk attachment and whip until stiff peaks form. Transfer the meringue to a piping bag fitted with a large St. Honoré piping tip (Ateco 881, 882, or 883). Pipe ribbons of meringue in a decorative manner on top of the pie. Use a torch to toast the meringue, if desired.

Pro Tips & Storage

- The pie can be kept in an airtight container or wrapped in plastic wrap for up to 5 days in the refrigerator.
- If you can't find pandan, you can make it without for a delicious salty lime meringue pie.
- If you opt out of using gelatin, it will still work, but it won't be as firm. It will keep for up to 3 days in the refrigerator.
- You can turn this into a lemon meringue pie by substituting lemon juice for the lime juice.
- Try making a yuzu meringue pie by substituting Yuzu Curd (page 141) for the pandan-lime curd.

Mango-Yakult Tres Leches Cake

Yakult is a Japanese yogurt probiotic drink that is very popular through-out Asia. It has a sweet but delicate and tangy flavor that is extremely refreshing. It was one of my favorite drinks as a child and is currently one of my favorite flavor inspirations. For this recipe, I have highlighted its floral and tangy notes by using it as the soak for a classic Mexican tres leches cake. Because there is no fat in the sponge cake itself, it allows for a very dry cake that is sturdy enough to absorb the milks without becoming soggy.

YIELD: Makes one 8½ by 4½ in [21.5 by 11 cm] loaf

CAKE

¾ cup + 1 Tbsp [120 g] all-purpose flour

1½ tsp baking powder

¼ tsp kosher salt

3 large eggs

⅔ cup [130 g] granulated sugar

1 tsp vanilla extract

3 Tbsp whole milk

3 Tbsp Yakult

SOAK

1½ cups [360 ml] Yakult

¾ cup [180 ml] sweetened condensed milk

½ cup [120 ml] heavy cream

TOPPING

¾ cup [180 ml] heavy cream

1 Tbsp powdered sugar

½ tsp vanilla extract

2 large mangoes, ripe but firm

1 Preheat the oven to 350°F [180°C] with a rack in the lower third. Grease a 8½ by 4½ in [21.5 by 11 cm] standard loaf pan with nonstick spray or butter and line the bottom with parchment paper. Set aside.

2 To make the cake, in a medium mixing bowl, whisk together the flour, baking powder, and salt. Set aside.

3 In the bowl of a stand mixer fitted with the whisk attachment, add the eggs and sugar. Whisk on high speed until light and fluffy, about 5 minutes. Add the vanilla.

4 Turn off the stand mixer and switch to a paddle attachment. Add about a third of the flour mixture to the bowl and mix on medium-low speed until barely combined, about 10 seconds. Stop the machine and scrape down the sides of the bowl. Pour in the whole milk. Paddle until just combined.

5 Add another third of the flour mixture and mix until just combined. Stop the machine, scrape down the sides of the bowl, and add the Yakult. Mix, then finish with the last third of the flour and mix until completely incorporated.

6 Pour the batter into the prepared loaf pan and smooth the top with a small offset spatula. Lightly tap the pan on the counter to remove any air bubbles. Bake for 30 to 35 minutes, until the cake pulls away from the sides of the pan and the top springs back to the touch. Remove from the oven and let cool for at least 30 minutes.

7 Meanwhile, make the soak. In a medium mixing bowl, whisk together the Yakult, sweetened condensed milk, and heavy cream.

8 Once the cake has cooled, carefully invert the loaf pan onto a cutting board. Peel off the parchment paper and trim the domed side of the cake so it can sit flush on a platter. Place the cake back in the pan with the freshly trimmed side up. Use a fork to poke holes all over the top of the cake, then pour the soak all over the top. Cover and let the cake soak in the fridge for at least 8 hours or overnight.

cont'd

9 To make the topping, in the bowl of a stand mixer fitted with the whisk attachment, whip together the **heavy cream**, **powdered sugar**, and **vanilla** until stiff peaks form. Do not overwhip, or the cream will curdle. Transfer to a piping bag fitted with a large St. Honoré piping tip (Ateco 883; see Pro Tips if you don't have one).

10 Peel the **mangoes** using a vegetable peeler. Slice the fleshy part off either side of the pit and lay them flat on the cutting board. Thinly slice each piece into ⅛ in [3 mm] thick slices. Set aside.

11 Remove the cake from the fridge and carefully invert onto a serving platter. Pipe ribbons of whipped cream on top, parallel to the shorter side of the cake. Arrange the mango slices by overlapping them decoratively on top of the whipped cream.

Pro Tips & Storage

- The finished cake can be stored in an airtight container for up to 4 days in the refrigerator.

- The baked, soaked cake can be wrapped in plastic wrap and stored for up to 3 months in the freezer.

- Try swapping the mango out for lychees, strawberries, or pineapple.

- If you don't have a St. Honoré piping tip, here's an easy hack: Take a disposable piping bag and cut the tip off, leaving ½ in [13 mm] wide opening. With the piping bag still folded in half, mark a dot ⅛ in [3 mm] inward from the opening you just cut. Mark a dot 1 in [2.5 cm] up the side of the piping bag. Connect the two dots and cut along that line.

Ube Chiffon Roll

Ube is one of the most iconic foods of the Philippines. This naturally violet-hued sweet potato is used in both savory and sweet applications. As a child, I remember always wanting to get the ube-flavored ice cream because purple was, and still is, my favorite color, but for some reason my mother had a vendetta against this marshmallowy, coconutty root and insisted I would not enjoy it. I didn't actually taste it until I was an adult and free of my mother's odd food opinions and discovered that, much to her dismay, I love it!

I decided to fill the cake with leche flan, another staple in Filipino cuisine. This cake is surprisingly light and perfect for special occasions or any night of the week.

YIELD: Makes 8 servings

COCONUT LECHE FLAN

¾ cup [150 g] granulated sugar

One 14 oz [415 ml] can sweetened condensed milk

One 13.5 oz [400 ml] can full-fat coconut milk

8 large egg yolks

3 large eggs

½ tsp kosher salt

UBE CHIFFON CAKE

4 large egg whites

¼ tsp kosher salt

½ cup + 2 Tbsp [130 g] granulated sugar

4 large egg yolks

1 Tbsp coconut oil or vegetable oil

3 Tbsp + 2 tsp [55 ml] full-fat coconut milk or whole milk

¾ cup + 1 Tbsp [100 g] cake flour, sifted

½ tsp baking powder

½ tsp ube extract

UBE CREAM

2 cups [480 ml] heavy cream

¼ cup [30 g] powdered sugar

1 drop ube extract

½ cup canned jackfruit in syrup, drained, patted dry, and cut into ¼ in [6 mm] strips (optional)

1 Preheat the oven to 375°F [190°C].

2 To make the coconut leche flan, in a small pot, combine the **sugar** with 3 Tbsp of water. Give it a stir and cook over medium-high heat to caramelize until medium amber brown, about 15 minutes. Pour the caramel into a 6 in [15 cm] square pan and allow to sit at room temp for 10 minutes before placing it in the freezer for another 15 minutes to harden.

3 Meanwhile, place the **condensed milk, coconut milk, egg yolks, eggs,** and **salt** in a blender. Blend on low speed until smooth, about 30 seconds. Strain through a fine-mesh sieve over the hardened caramel in the pan.

4 Set up a water bath by placing the flan pan inside a larger baking pan. Add boiling water until halfway up the sides of the flan pan and bake until just set, 50 to 55 minutes. The flan should still be slightly jiggly in the center. Remove the pan from the water bath and allow to cool for 1 hour before placing the pan in the refrigerator to chill completely, about 4 hours.

5 To make the ube cake, preheat the oven to 350°F [180°C]. In the bowl of a stand mixer fitted with the whisk attachment, combine the **egg whites** and **salt.** Whisk on medium speed until frothy, then add the **sugar** in three additions, with about 30 seconds in between. Continue to whip on high speed until stiff peaks form, 2 to 3 minutes. Set aside.

6 In a large mixing bowl, combine the **egg yolks** and **coconut oil** and whisk to combine. Add the **coconut milk** and whisk again until smooth.

cont'd

Add the flour, baking powder, and ube extract and mix until no streaks remain.

7   To lighten the batter, add about one third of the egg whites to the batter and fold using a whisk. Add another third and gently fold it in with as few strokes as possible to combine. Add the final third and fold until no streaks remain and you have a silky smooth but aerated batter.

8   Line a 9 by 13 in [23 by 33 cm] baking sheet with parchment paper. Pour in the batter and smooth out to an even layer, making sure to get into the corners and all way to the edges of the pan. Bake until the cake is cooked through and bounces back to the touch, 25 to 30 minutes. Allow to cool completely in the pan.

9   Carefully unmold the flan onto a large plate. You may have to loosen the edges with a paring knife and/or tilt the pan to the side and run the bottom of the pan under hot water.

Transfer the flan to a cutting board and pat dry using paper towels. Try to soak up as much moisture from all sides of the flan as possible so it doesn't bleed into the cream inside the cake.

10 Cut two 1½ x 6 in [4 cm] strips of flan. Cut one of those strips in half so it measures 3 in [7.5 cm] long. Reserve the leftover flan to munch or cut into little cubes to garnish.

11 To make the ube cream, in the bowl of a stand mixer fitted with the whisk attachment, combine the heavy cream and powdered sugar. Whip, starting on medium-low speed and moving up to high speed, until stiff peaks form. Add the ube extract and mix until the color is uniform. Do not overwhip.

12 Loosen the edges of the ube cake with a paring knife and turn the cake out onto a cutting board. Peel off the parchment paper and place the cake with the same side down onto the center of a fresh sheet of

parchment paper roughly measuring 12 by 16 in [30.5 by 40.5 cm]. With the short side of the cake facing you, spread on a ½ in [13 mm] thick layer of the ube cream. Scatter with sliced jackfruit, if using. Place the remaining ube cream in a piping bag fitted with a decorative tip such as a St. Honoré, French star, or plain round. Keep refrigerated until ready to use.

13 Place one full strip plus the 3 in [7.5 cm] long strip of flan against the short edge of the cake closest to you. With the help of the parchment paper, carefully roll it up to form a tight log. Keep it wrapped tightly in the parchment paper and place it seam-side down in the refrigerator to chill for at least 30 minutes.

14 Unwrap the cake and carefully place it onto a cutting board. Slice about ½ in [13 mm] off each end of the roll for a cleaner look. Transfer the cake to a serving platter, pipe more ube cream on the top of the cake

cont'd

in a decorative fashion, and garnish with the reserved flan cubes and/or more strips of jackfruit. Slice and serve.

Pro Tips & Storage

- The fully assembled cake can be stored in an airtight container or loosely wrapped in plastic wrap for up to 4 days in the refrigerator.

- The cake can be made in advance and stored wrapped in plastic wrap for up to 4 days in the refrigerator or 3 months in the freezer.

- The flan can be made in advance and stored in an airtight container or wrapped in plastic wrap for up to 4 days in the refrigerator.

- If you want to serve the flan plain, it can be made in individual molds or round- or oval-shaped pans. The main purpose of making it in the square-shaped pan is to form strips to fit inside the cake roll. If you are serving the flan plain, turn it out directly onto a serving platter and keep all the yummy caramel juices; do not pat it dry.

- Ube extract is very concentrated, so be careful when measuring, otherwise you'll end up with a cake and cream that look like Grimace.

Honey-Yuzu Caked Alaska

On a trip to St. Petersburg, Russia, I saw beautifully executed cakes, meringues, and confections all made in the classic way but with their own distinctive style. And there was color, lots of color—naturally hued pinks and greens and golds. One of the desserts I became fascinated with was the medovik, with its numerous pencil-thin layers of honey cake and sour cream. The layers were so perfect and uniform, and the cake itself tasted like honey scraped fresh out of a honeycomb balanced with the perfect tang.

The flavor reminded me of Korean honey citron tea. And so, as I do, I created my own version of a medovik layered with yuzu, an Asian fruit that tastes of lemon, lime, and mandarin orange, and covered with toasted meringue—a "caked" Alaska if you will.

YIELD: Makes 8 servings

HONEY CAKE

½ cup + 3 Tbsp [160 g] unsalted butter

⅔ cup [130 g] granulated sugar

¼ cup [85 g] honey

2 large eggs

2¼ cups [340 g] all-purpose flour

½ tsp kosher salt

½ tsp baking soda

YUZU CURD

1½ tsp powdered gelatin

1¼ cups [250 g] granulated sugar

1 cup [240 ml] yuzu juice

4 large eggs

2 large egg yolks

1¼ cups [280 g] unsalted butter, cubed, cold

½ tsp kosher salt

3 recipes Swiss Meringue (page 157)

1   To make the honey cake, in a small pot over medium heat, melt the butter and continue to cook until amber brown, about 15 minutes.

2   Transfer the butter to a large mixing bowl and add the sugar and honey. Whisk until smooth. Whisk in the eggs one at a time. Then add the flour, salt, and baking soda and stir until completely combined and no lumps remain. Form the dough into a flat rectangle, wrap in plastic wrap, and place in the refrigerator to chill for 1 hour.

3   Meanwhile, make the yuzu curd. In a small dish, add 1 Tbsp of water and sprinkle over the gelatin. Quickly stir to combine and set aside to bloom.

4   In a small pot, whisk together the sugar, yuzu juice, and eggs. Cook over medium-high heat, whisking continuously, until thickened, about 8 minutes. Remove from the heat and add the bloomed gelatin. Whisk until completely dissolved.

5   Strain the curd through a fine-mesh sieve over a medium bowl to remove any egg or gelatin bits. Add the cubed butter and salt. Whisk to melt the butter slightly then use a stick blender (or a regular blender on low speed) to finish emulsifying the curd until silky smooth.

6   Place a piece of plastic wrap directly on the surface of the curd to prevent a skin from forming. Place the bowl over an ice bath to cool for 30 minutes before transferring it to the refrigerator to chill for 1 hour.

7   Cut two sheets of parchment paper measuring 12 by 16 in [30.5 by 40.5 cm]. Cut the dough in half and place one piece between the sheets of parchment. Roll out the dough into a rectangle at least 9 by 16 in [23 by 40.5 cm] and ⅛ in [3 mm] thick. Place on a tray in the refrigerator or freezer to chill for 30 minutes. Repeat with the other half of the dough.

8   Preheat the oven to 350°F [180°C]. Line two 13 by 17 in [33 by 43 cm] baking sheets with parchment paper.

cont'd

9 Take one sheet of dough and peel off one side of the parchment, gently lay it back on the dough, flip, and peel off the other side. Cut each sheet of dough into four rectangles measuring 4 by 8 in [10 by 20 cm], placing them on the prepared baking sheets. If you don't get enough on the first round, you can gather the scraps and reroll them one more time as before to make up for any missing pieces.

10 Bake the layers until amber brown, 15 minutes. Allow to cool completely on the baking sheets.

11 Stir the yuzu curd to loosen it up a bit. Place one layer of honey cake on a serving platter and spread a ¼ in [6 mm] thick layer of curd on top. Place another layer of cake on top of the curd and repeat until all eight layers are used. Place in the fridge to chill while you make the meringue.

12 You will need to make a triple recipe of Swiss meringue. It sounds like a lot, but you will probably use most if not all of it.

13 Immediately cover the entire cake with the meringue with flowy, swirly strokes and a copious amount on top. It should look organic and free flowing with some nice peaks on the top. The more dimension, the better for torching. Use a blow torch to toast the meringue. Refrigerate for at least 4 hours before serving to help the curd reset and soften up the cake layers.

Pro Tips & Storage

- The fully assembled cake can be stored in an airtight container or loosely wrapped in plastic wrap for up to 4 days in the refrigerator.

- The assembled cake minus the meringue can be made one day and frosted with the meringue the next. In this case, you can serve it immediately.

- The cake dough can be kept wrapped in plastic wrap or rolled between parchment for up to 4 days in the refrigerator or 3 months in the freezer.

- The yuzu curd can be kept in an airtight container for up to 1 week in the refrigerator.

- Yuzu juice is often sold as "yuzu extract" in bottles on the shelf in Asian markets. If you can't find yuzu juice or extract, you can substitute lemon juice or a combination of lemon, lime, and orange juice in the same amount.

Ispahan Jelly Cake

Ispahan is a flavor combination of raspberry, rose, and lychees. The term was coined by the legendary French pastry chef Pierre Hermé in homage to the fragrant roses of the city of Isfahan in Iran. I first tried ispahan while living in Paris in the form of a macaron from Hermé's shop, and I was instantly obsessed. What a beautifully light, subtle, and aromatic melding of ingredients, each one dancing with the next.

I made a version of this cake on a baking competition show, and the judges loved it. It strikes a perfect harmony between French, Asian, and Middle Eastern baking cultures. I did not end up winning the show, but I took this dessert with me, which is a win in my book.

YIELD: Makes one 8 in [20 cm] cake

BISCUIT JOCONDE

3 large egg whites

⅔ cup [130 g] granulated sugar

4 large eggs

1¼ cups [150 g] blanched almond flour, sifted

3 Tbsp all-purpose flour

¼ tsp kosher salt

2 Tbsp raspberry preserves

1 cup [120 g] fresh raspberries

RASPBERRY-ROSE MOUSSE

Two 20 oz [600 ml] can lychees in heavy syrup

1½ tsp powdered gelatin

1 cup [120 g] raspberries, fresh or frozen, thawed

1 lemon, juice only

2 Tbsp granulated sugar

¼ tsp kosher salt

½ cup [120 ml] heavy cream, cold

¼ tsp rose water (optional)

COCONUT JELLY

4 cups [960 ml] coconut water

¼ cup + 2 Tbsp [80 g] granulated sugar

1 Tbsp agar agar powder or 2 Tbsp + 1 tsp powdered gelatin (see Pro Tips)

1 Preheat the oven to 375°F [190°C]. Grease a 9 by 13 in [23 by 33 cm] baking sheet and line it with parchment paper.

2 To make the biscuit joconde, in the bowl of a stand mixer fitted with the whisk attachment, whip the egg whites on medium speed until frothy. Increase the speed to medium-high and add ⅓ cup [65 g] of the sugar in three additions with about 30 seconds in between until the meringue forms medium-stiff peaks, 2 to 3 minutes. Transfer to a bowl. Do not wash out the mixer bowl or whisk attachment.

3 In the same bowl of the stand mixer, place the eggs and the remaining ⅓ cup [65 g] of sugar. Whisk on medium-high speed until the eggs are pale, fluffy, and have tripled in volume, 3 to 5 minutes.

4 Remove the bowl from the mixer and whisk in by hand the almond flour, all-purpose flour, and salt. Add about one third of the meringue and fold it in with the whisk to loosen the batter. Add another third and fold, then the last third and fold it in until no streaks remain.

5 Pour the batter into the prepared baking sheet and spread it out into a smooth and even layer. Bake until the cake is golden brown around the edges and bounces back to the touch, 18 to 20 minutes. Allow the cake to cool in the sheet for a half hour before transferring to the refrigerator to chill for another hour.

6 Line the wall of a 7 in [18 cm] springform pan or cake ring with acetate. The acetate should be at least 3½ in [9 cm] high and overlap by at least 1 in [2.5 cm]. Tape the seam shut on the inside all the way to the bottom. Turn the cake out onto a cutting board and peel off the parchment paper. Cut the cake into two strips lengthwise, 2 in [5 cm] wide each. Take one strip and place it against the acetate around the wall of the ring. Take the other strip and trim it to fill the

cont'd

empty space so you have a full wall of cake. Take the leftover cake and piece it together, pressing it into the base, making sure to fill the bottom of the pan completely.

7   Spread the raspberry preserves on the cake in the bottom of the pan and then top with the raspberries. Place it in the freezer to chill.

8   To make the raspberry-rose mousse, drain the lychees, reserving 2 Tbsp of the syrup from the can. Pour the syrup into a small bowl and sprinkle the gelatin on top. Quickly whisk together to form a gross gelatinous lump. Set aside to bloom. Using a paper towel, pat the drained lychees dry, then transfer them to a paper towel–lined airtight container and refrigerate until step 16.

9   In a blender, combine the raspberries and lemon juice. Purée until smooth. To remove the seeds, strain through a fine-mesh sieve into a small pot, making sure to squeeze out every last drop of raspberry juice. Whisk in the sugar and salt and heat over medium-high heat until just before boiling and the sugar is dissolved. Add the gelatin mass and whisk until it is dissolved and no lumps remain. Pour the mixture into a large mixing bowl and allow it to cool to room temperature, 15 to 30 minutes. Do not let it start to set up, though.

10 In the bowl of a stand mixer fitted with the whisk attachment, whip the heavy cream and rose water, if using, until stiff peaks form. Do not overwhip.

11 Add about one third of the whipped cream to the raspberry purée and gently fold it in using a whisk. Add another third of the cream and fold, trying not to deflate the mousse. Add in the final third and fold, using as few strokes as possible, until no streaks remain.

12 Pour the mousse into the cake, smooth out the top, and freeze for at least 6 hours or overnight.

13 To make the coconut jelly, in a small pot, place 2 cups [480 ml] of the coconut water and bring it to a boil. While it's heating, whisk together the sugar and agar agar. Once the coconut water comes to a rolling boil, pour in the sugar and agar agar mixture and whisk until everything is dissolved. Remove from the heat and transfer to a large pitcher or bowl with a pouring spout (something that makes your life easier when you pour it over the cake).

cont'd

14 Whisk in the remaining 2 cups [480 ml] of coconut water and allow the mixture to cool to room temperature, about 30 minutes. Agar agar sets up very fast, so if your house is on the colder side, keep an eye on it. You want the liquid to be as cool as possible without it setting up at all.

15 While the jelly is cooling, line the wall of an 8 in [20 cm] springform pan or cake ring with acetate. If using a springform pan, only use the ring part. The acetate should be at least 3½ in [9 cm] high and overlap by at least 1 in [2.5 cm]. Tape the seam shut on the inside all the way to the bottom. Place the cake ring on a serving platter. Use tape (I use masking or waterproof) to tape shut the seam where the ring meets the plate, going all the way around. You want a tight seal so the liquid jelly doesn't leak out.

16 Gather the lychees from step 8. Cut each one into a few smaller pieces; they should naturally look like flower petals.

17 Remove the mousse cake from the freezer, unmold it, and remove the acetate. Place the frozen cake in the center of the larger cake ring. Arrange the lychee "petals" over the top of the mousse so it looks like a flower. Pour a little of the coconut jelly liquid between the walls of the cake and cake ring first. If it starts to leak out the sides, you need to tape it better. Once you know the cake is sealed and secured, pour it all the way to the top and over the top of the cake. Place it in the refrigerator to finish setting, about 1 hour. Remove the tape, cake ring, and acetate, then slice and serve chilled.

Pro Tips & Storage

- The fully assembled cake can be stored in an airtight container or loosely wrapped in plastic wrap for up to 4 days in the refrigerator.

- The cake without the jelly can be made in advance and stored, wrapped in plastic wrap, for up to 3 months in the freezer.

- I highly recommend using agar agar. Since gelatin sets up quickly and firmly, the cake won't be able to absorb as much liquid as if you use it. You can find agar agar in every Asian market, and it's easily available online too. But if you really prefer to use powdered gelatin, remove ¼ cup [60 ml] of coconut water from the pot in step 13 and pour it into a shallow dish or bowl. Sprinkle the gelatin over it and quickly whisk to form a mass. Heat the rest of the coconut water in the pot with the sugar until dissolved and just before boiling. Whisk in the gelatin mass and proceed to step 14.

- You can also frost the cake with vanilla buttercream (see page 176; substitute 1 tsp of vanilla extract for the Ovaltine). Frosting with buttercream will create a barrier between the cake and the jelly if you don't want the cake to absorb it. If you go this route, after frosting the cake you should freeze it for at least two hours before pouring on the jelly, so the buttercream won't melt and bleed.

- If you want to get real fancy, you can garnish a few tips of the lychee "petals" with gold leaf.

- All of these recipes are great on their own. You can use the joconde recipe to make a three-layer cake; make the mousse in individual cups and top with lychees or other fresh fruit; or make the jelly in a pan and cut into small cubes to serve in drinks, on top of shaved ice, or with other desserts.

Almond Dofu Charlotte
Ladyfinger Cake with Almond Jelly

One of my favorite Chinese desserts as a kid was almond dofu, or almond jelly. Traditionally it isn't made with almonds at all but instead with apricot kernels, just like our Italian friends, amaretto liqueur and amaretti cookies. This recipe is my take on a Charlotte Russe, a cake made with a wall of ladyfingers and filled with Bavarian cream and berries. In my version, it is instead filled with almond dofu, fresh balled melon, and yes, maraschino cherries, because any excuse to put them in a dessert is a fantastic one. If you're a hater and want to use fresh pitted cherries, that would be delicious, too. It is such a light and refreshing dish, perfect any time of the year, but especially good in hot, humid months.

YIELD: Makes one 6 in [15 cm] cake

LADYFINGER CAKE

4 large egg whites

⅔ cup [130 g] granulated sugar

4 large egg yolks

⅔ cup [100 g] all-purpose flour

3 Tbsp potato starch or cornstarch

1 tsp vanilla extract

½ tsp kosher salt

1 Tbsp powdered sugar

1 cup [150 g] white chocolate chunks

ALMOND DOFU

¼ cup + 2 Tbsp [80 g] granulated sugar

1¼ tsp agar agar powder or 1 Tbsp powdered gelatin (see Pro Tips)

1½ cups [360 ml] whole milk, cold

1 Tbsp almond extract

¼ tsp kosher salt

¾ cup [100 g] cantaloupe melon balls

¾ cup [100 g] honeydew melon balls

¾ cup [100 g] maraschino cherries or fresh pitted cherries

1 Preheat the oven to 350°F [180°C].

2 To make the ladyfinger cake, in the bowl of a stand mixer fitted with the whisk attachment, whip the **egg whites** on medium speed until frothy. Increase the speed to medium-high and add ⅓ cup [65 g] of the **sugar** in three additions with about 30 seconds in between until the meringue forms stiff peaks, 2 to 3 minutes. Transfer to a bowl. Do not wash out the mixer bowl or whisk attachment.

3 In the same bowl of the stand mixer place the **egg yolks** and remaining ⅓ cup [65 g] of sugar. Whisk on medium-high until the eggs are pale and fluffy, about 2 minutes.

4 Take the bowl off the mixer and whisk in by hand the **flour, potato starch, vanilla,** and **salt.** Add about one third of the meringue and fold it in with the whisk to loosen the batter. Add another third and fold it in, trying not to deflate the batter, then the last third and fold it in until no streaks remain. Make sure you start with stiff peaks on the meringue and do not overmix. The batter should be stiff enough to hold its shape when piped. You

have to be extra attentive to this step because if it's overmixed and the batter doesn't hold its shape, you are SOL and will have to start over. Transfer the batter to a piping bag fitted with a ½ in [13 mm] circle tip.

5 Cut a sheet of parchment paper measuring at least 12 by 16 in [30.5 by 40.5 cm]. Fold it in half lengthwise and fold the seam edge down ½ in [13 mm]. Measure 5 in [13 cm] down and fold lengthwise along that line. Open up the parchment paper, and you should now have a guide for two 5 in [13 cm] rows. Place it on a 13 by 17 in [33 by 43 cm] baking sheet.

6 Pipe two rows of vertical stripes of batter directly touching each other and going across the guides like a picket fence. Using a fine-mesh sieve, dust the tops with **powdered sugar.** Bake until slightly darker around the edges and cooked through, 15 minutes. Allow to cool completely on the baking sheet.

cont'd

7 Line the inside wall of a 6 in [15 cm] springform pan or cake ring with acetate or parchment paper and tape the seam together. Place on a serving plate.

8 Trim as little as possible off the bottom of the ladyfinger fence so it can sit flush in the pan. Carefully peel off one row of ladyfingers and place it around the inside of the ring. Carefully cut enough from the second row of ladyfingers to fill the gap. Piece together the leftover cake and press it into the bottom in one layer, making sure there are no gaps.

9 In a small bowl, melt the white chocolate in the microwave in 30 second increments, stirring in between, until melted. Use a silicone brush or the back of a spoon to paint a thin layer on the entire inside of the cake with the melted chocolate, especially in the seams. This will act as a seal so the almond jelly won't soak through the cake. Place the cake in the freezer to chill.

10 To make the almond dofu, in a small pot, bring 1½ cups [360 ml] of water to a rolling boil. While it's heating, in a small bowl, whisk together the sugar and agar agar. Drizzle the mixture into the boiling water and whisk until completely dissolved.

11 Transfer to a large pitcher or bowl with a pouring spout. Add the cold milk, almond extract, and salt. Whisk to combine. Allow to cool for 15 minutes.

12 Meanwhile, prepare the fruit. Scoop melon balls out of the cantaloupe and honeydew. Place them on a paper towel to dry. Drain and stem the maraschino cherries and pat them dry with a paper towel.

13 Reserve about one third of each fruit for the garnish. Place the rest on the inside of the chilled cake. Pour the almond dofu into the cake up to ½ in [13 mm] below the top. Place in the refrigerator to chill completely, about 1 hour.

14 Carefully unmold the cake, then garnish with the reserved fruit, slice, and serve.

Pro Tips & Storage

- The fully assembled cake can be stored in an airtight container or loosely wrapped in plastic wrap for up to 4 days in the refrigerator.

- I highly recommend using agar agar. Since gelatin sets up quickly and firmly, the cake won't be able to absorb as much liquid as if you use it. You can find agar agar in every Asian market, and it's easily available online too. But if you really prefer to use powdered gelatin, remove ½ cup [120 ml] of the water from the pot in step 10 and pour it into a shallow dish or bowl. Sprinkle the gelatin over it and quickly whisk to form a mass. Heat the rest of the water in the pot with the sugar until dissolved and just before boiling. Whisk in the gelatin mass and proceed to step 11.

- You can also make this almond dofu without the cake and pour it directly into a pan. Cut it into cubes once set and add a fresh fruit cocktail to the top for a refreshing treat.

- This is a great, versatile ladyfinger recipe that can be used for many other bakes, such as tiramisu.

Mango Sticky Rice Cake

This cake combines two of my favorite desserts: mango pudding and mango sticky rice. There's a restaurant in Hong Kong, Hui Lau Shan, that focuses on all things mango. If there's a way to cook it, cut it, or serve it, this place knows the answer. Every time we visited, my sister and I always ordered the "Many Mango" as we pointed to the bright blue poster of the most beautiful arrangement of mango prepared in every which way known to man.

This restaurant ignited my mango obsession and eventually led me to creating this dessert: a firm-yet-chewy shell of sweet coconut sticky rice filled with silky and sweet mango pudding and chunks of refreshing mango. It's the perfect treat whether outside on beautiful summer day or stuck inside during a rainstorm.

YIELD: Makes one 6 in [15 cm] cake

COCONUT STICKY RICE

¾ cup + 2 Tbsp [170 g] Thai sticky rice

2 cups + 2 Tbsp [515 ml] boiling water

¼ cup + 1 Tbsp [75 ml] full-fat coconut milk

1 Tbsp + 2 tsp granulated sugar

¼ tsp kosher salt

MANGO PUDDING

4 to 6 champagne, honey, or Manila mangoes (depending on the size), plus 1 for garnish (optional)

½ cup [100 g] granulated sugar

1 lemon, juice only

1 Tbsp + 2½ tsp powdered gelatin

1½ cups + 1 Tbsp [375 ml] full-fat coconut milk, cold

¼ tsp kosher salt

1   To make the coconut sticky rice, in a heatproof mixing bowl, place the **sticky rice** and pour the **boiling water** over it. Give it a stir and cover with a tea towel for 30 minutes to soak.

2   Strain the rice through a fine-mesh sieve over a bowl. Wash the rice with tepid water until it runs clear to get rid of the starches. Line a steamer basket with a wet steamer cloth or banana leaf and bring the water to a boil. If you don't have a steamer setup, you can place a thin tea towel inside a metal colander that completely fits inside a larger pot filled with 2 in [5 cm] of water.

3   Place the washed rice into the steamer basket and make a well in the center. Fold the corners of the towel over the rice and steam for 20 minutes.

4   Meanwhile, in a liquid measuring cup, whisk together the **coconut milk, sugar,** and **salt.**

5   Remove the steamer basket from the boiling water and fluff the rice with a fork. Pour the coconut milk mixture over the rice and carefully stir until all the liquid is absorbed. Cover and let it sit for 5 minutes.

6   Line the bottom of a 6 in [15 cm] springform pan or cake ring with parchment paper. Press the sticky rice into an even layer at the bottom of the pan, making sure to press firmly and all the way up to the edges. This will create a seal so the pudding doesn't leak through. Cover with plastic wrap and refrigerate until ready to use.

7   To make the mango pudding, peel and cut the flesh off 4 to 6 of the **mangoes.** Place in a blender and process to a smooth purée. Measure out 1¾ cups [420 ml] of purée (reserve any remaining for another purpose) and place it in a small pot with ½ cup [120 ml] of water, the **sugar,** and the **lemon juice.** Whisk together over medium-high heat and bring to a scald—small bubbles around the edges, right before boiling.

8   Meanwhile, in a small dish, quickly whisk together ¼ cup + 2 Tbsp [90 ml] of water and the **gelatin** to form a goop. Allow it to bloom while the purée is heating.

cont'd

9 Add the lump of gelatin to the purée and whisk until completely dissolved and no lumps remain. Remove from the heat and pour through a fine-mesh sieve into a bowl or pitcher. Whisk in the **coconut milk** and **salt**. Allow to cool until just warm to the touch, 10 to 20 minutes.

10 Meanwhile, cut one of the mangoes into ½ in [13 mm] dice; you should have about ¾ cup [100 g]. Place them on top of the sticky rice crust. Pour the cooled mango pudding into the cake ring. Place in the refrigerator to completely set, about 4 hours.

11 Carefully unmold the cake and transfer to a platter to serve. Peel the last mango and cut it into ½ in [13 mm] cubes to garnish, if desired.

Pro Tips & Storage

- The fully assembled cake can be stored in an airtight container or loosely wrapped in plastic wrap for up to 4 days in the refrigerator.

- The coconut sticky rice is great on its own or with sliced fresh mangoes in a more traditional fashion. Simply serve after step 5.

- The mango pudding is also great on its own. You can pour it into a large jelly mold or individual cups. Top with condensed or evaporated milk and more fresh mango chunks for a light and refreshing treat.

- Some Asian and Latin markets have mango purée in the freezer section. It usually comes in old-school frozen concentrated juice cans or bags. If you can find it, I recommend using it for this recipe.

Passion Fruit Mille Feuille

I was 25 years old when I lived in Paris and had the privilege of living on one of the city's most iconic streets, Rue St. Honoré, in the 1st arrondissement. I had just gone through a terrible breakup and badly needed some comfort. Luckily for me, I lived across the street from an incredible bakery. They sold the most amazing everything, but their mille feuilles specifically provided me with the most comfort—a hug in the form of the perfect bite. A thousand layers of flaky and tender pastry surrounded the creamiest crème pâtissière; each bite left me feeling like I was floating in the clouds.

YIELD: Makes 6 to 8 servings

PUFF PASTRY

1⅓ cups [200 g] all-purpose flour

¾ cup [170 g] unsalted butter, at room temperature

½ tsp kosher salt

⅓ cup [80 ml] cold water

¼ cup [80 g] light corn syrup

PASSION FRUIT CREMEUX

1 cup [240 g] passion fruit purée or pulp, seedless or strained (see Pro Tips for substitutions)

5 large egg yolks

3 Tbsp granulated sugar

2 tsp powdered gelatin

⅓ cup [50 g] white chocolate chunks

5 Tbsp [70 g] unsalted butter, at room temperature

¼ tsp kosher salt

SWISS MERINGUE

4 large egg whites

¾ cup + 2 Tbsp [180 g] granulated sugar

¼ tsp kosher salt

Passion fruit seeds, for garnish (optional)

1 To make the puff pastry, in the bowl of a stand mixer fitted with the paddle attachment, mix together the **flour**, 2 Tbsp of the **butter**, and the **salt** until it resembles a coarse meal, 2 to 3 minutes. Slowly stream in the **cold water** until it turns into a shaggy mass that will hold when squeezed together. If the dough is still dry, add cold water, 1 tsp at a time, until it holds together. Pat the dough into a flat square on a piece of plastic wrap and place in the refrigerator for 1 hour to chill. Do not wash out the mixer bowl.

2 In the same mixer bowl, place the remaining ½ cup + 2 Tbsp [135 g] of butter and paddle until smooth, 30 seconds. Scrape out the butter onto a sheet of parchment paper. Fold the paper over the butter and, using a rolling pin, roll it out to an even 4 by 6 in [10 by 15 cm] rectangle. You can fold up the edges at the exact measurements to create a clean looking butter block. Set aside at room temperature.

3 To make the passion fruit cremeux, measure out the **passion fruit purée** into a small pot and remove 2 Tbsp into a small dish. Add the **egg yolks** and **sugar** to the pot and whisk to combine.

4 Sprinkle the **gelatin** over the reserved passion fruit purée and quickly mix into a gelatinous blob. Set aside to bloom.

5 Place the pot over medium-high heat and cook, whisking continuously, until thickened, 10 minutes. Add the bloomed gelatin and whisk until completely dissolved.

6 In a small mixing bowl, place the **white chocolate** and pour the passion fruit mixture over it through a fine-mesh sieve. Whisk until smooth. Add the **butter** and **salt** and emulsify with a stick blender (or a regular blender on low speed).

cont'd

7 Place a piece of plastic wrap directly touching the cremeux to prevent a skin from forming. Place the bowl over an ice bath to cool for 30 minutes before transferring it to the refrigerator to chill for at least 2 hours.

8 Place the butter block in the refrigerator for 10 minutes. Take out the dough and place it on a floured work surface. Sprinkle some flour on top of the dough and roll it out to an 8½ by 7 in [21.5 by 18 cm] rectangle with the long side facing you. It should be about ¼ in [6 mm] thick. Peel one side of the parchment off the butter block and place the block in the center of the dough, long side facing you, peeling off the rest of the parchment as you lay it down, like a Band-Aid.

9 Fold the top and bottom of the dough over the butter to meet in the center. Pinch the dough tightly together at the seam to seal. Pinch the two side edges closed so the butter is completely enclosed in the dough. The goal is to have the dough and butter at the same stiffness; if your butter starts oozing out all over the place when you are trying to do this, place it back in the refrigerator and wait until it is firm.

10 Carefully roll the block out to a rectangle, approximately 8 by 12 in [20 by 30.5 cm]. Fold it into thirds crosswise so it looks more like a square. Turn the dough block 90 degrees and roll it out again to a rectangle, 8 by 12 in [20 by 30.5 cm]. Then fold it into thirds once more. Wrap in plastic wrap and allow it to rest in the refrigerator for 30 minutes.

11 Repeat step 10 two more times.

12 Preheat the oven to 400°F [200°C] with racks in the top and bottom third. Take out the dough and let it sit for 5 minutes.

13 Flour a work surface and roll out the dough to an 11 by 15 in [28 by 38 cm] rectangle ⅛ in [3 mm] thick. Brush off any excess flour and carefully transfer the dough to a parchment-lined baking sheet. Place another sheet of parchment on top of the dough and three more baking sheets on top. The idea is to weigh the dough down so it doesn't rise. If you don't have that many, you can top it with one baking sheet and a casserole or whatever oven-proof dish you have.

14 Bake on the lower rack for 30 minutes. Remove from the oven and take off the top baking sheets. Peel off the parchment and, using two spatulas, carefully flip the dough over.

15 Using a pastry brush or silicone brush, brush about half of the **corn syrup** over the top of the puff pastry. Place it back in the oven on the top rack and bake until dark golden brown and blistered, 5 minutes.

16 Remove from the oven and carefully flip it over once more. Brush the top with the remaining corn syrup. Return to the top rack of the oven and bake until dark golden brown and blistered, 10 to 13 minutes more.

17 Straight from the oven, carefully transfer the sheet of puff pastry to a cutting board. Trim all four sides of the pastry to get straight edges. Cut it into thirds; you should get three rectangles measuring roughly 4 by 9 in [10 by 23 cm]. Allow them to cool completely on a tray or wire rack. It is important to cut the puff pastry while it's still hot or warm to get clean edges.

18 Remove the cremeux from the refrigerator and use a spatula to stir it until loosened and smooth. Transfer to a piping bag fitted with a ⅜ in [9.5 mm] circle piping tip (I used Ateco 805). Place one layer of puff pastry on a serving platter. Pipe kisses all over the top (4 across and 9 down), gently lay another layer of pastry on top of the cremeux, and place the pastry in the refrigerator while you make the Swiss meringue. Reserve any leftover cremeux to garnish, if desired.

19 In a medium pot, bring about 2 in [5 cm] of water to a boil. The pot should be big enough to hold the

bowl of a stand mixer on the rim without touching the water. Place the egg whites, sugar, and salt in the bowl of the stand mixer. Place the bowl over the pot and whisk continuously until it reaches 160°F [70°C], about 5 minutes This is to cook out any possible bacteria that may be in the raw eggs.

20 Place the bowl in the stand mixer fitted with the whisk attachment and whip until stiff peaks form. Transfer the meringue to a piping bag fitted with the same tip you used for the cremeux. Pipe kisses all over the top of the second layer of puff pastry (4 across and 9 down); and gently lay the final layer of puff pastry onto the meringue.

21 Use the rest of the meringue to pipe the top in a decorative manner. Garnish with dots of cremeux and passion fruit seeds, if desired. Place in the refrigerator to set for 4 hours or overnight before slicing.

Pro Tips & Storage

- The assembled mille feuille can be kept in an airtight container for up to 4 days in the refrigerator.

- The puff pastry dough can be made in advance and kept wrapped in plastic wrap for up to 3 days in the refrigerator or 3 months in the freezer.

- The cremeux can be stored in an airtight container for up to 5 days in the refrigerator.

- The meringue should be made when you are ready to use it.

- Mille feuilles are tricky to cut. I recommend using a serrated knife in a sawing motion.

- Passion fruit purée (sometimes called pulp) can often be found in good Latin markets or Asian markets in plastic pouches in the refrigerated or freezer section.

- If you can't find passion fruit anywhere, you can substitute mango purée in the same ratio with the juice of 1 lemon.

- Try swapping out the passion fruit cremeux and/or meringue for Corn Custard (page 79), Mascarpone Cream (page 114), Pastry Cream (page 117), Matcha Cream (page 125), Pandan-Lime Curd (page 129), Yuzu Curd (page 141), Ube Cream (page 135), Ovaltine Buttercream (page 176), Ovaltine Ganache (page 174), Stabilized Malted Chantilly (page 175), Raspberry Ganache (page 188), Horlicks Ganache (page 192), or Royal Milk Tea Diplomat (page 204).

Macau Egg Tart Pâtissier

When I was 10 years old, we stayed in one of the most iconic buildings of the HK skyline, the Shun Tak Centre. At the base of the building was the ferry terminal where you could catch a hydrofoil to Macau, which was once a Portuguese colony and popularized one of Portugal's most famous desserts: the pastel de nata, egg custard tarts. They made their way to Hong Kong but evolved into a uncaramelized version called dan tat, which can be found in every Chinese bakery. The egg tarts in Macau, however, stayed true to the original Portuguese version. Another of my favorites is the French flan pâtissier, which is made with puff pastry, where the whole top gets burnt. My version is a combination of all of the above, with a thin layer of hazelnut praliné between the crust and the custard for extra nuttiness.

YIELD: Makes one 9 in [23 cm] fluted tart

---

1 recipe Puff Pastry (page 157)

HAZELNUT PRALINÉ

¾ cup [90 g] hazelnuts

¼ cup + 2 Tbsp [80 g] granulated sugar

¼ tsp kosher salt

CUSTARD FILLING

2 large eggs

5 large egg yolks

3 Tbsp cornstarch

1 vanilla bean, seeds scraped, or 2 tsp vanilla extract

¼ tsp kosher salt

2 cups [480 ml] whole milk

¾ cup [180 ml] heavy cream

¾ cup [150 g] granulated sugar

1 Tbsp granulated sugar

1   Make the puff pastry steps 1 and 2, then steps 8 to 12.

2   Grease the inside of a 9 by 1¾ in [23 by 4.5 cm] fluted tart liberally with softened butter. Flour a work surface and roll the pastry dough out to a 14 in [35.5 cm] circle, ⅛ in

[3 mm] thick. Carefully drape the dough into the prepared tart shell, pressing into the bottom first, then up the sides. Do not pull or stretch the dough but allow it to lay in the mold fully relaxed, making sure to press it into the corners and crevices. Place the shell into the refrigerator for 10 minutes to firm up before using a paring knife to trim off the excess dough.

3   Preheat the oven to 400°F [200°C] with racks in the top and bottom thirds. Use a fork to dock holes in the bottom of the tart. Line the inside with a piece of parchment paper and baking weights, beans, or rice, then blind bake on the bottom rack for 20 minutes. Remove the paper and weights and dock holes into the bottom again, then bake on the top rack for 10 minutes more. Remove from the oven and set aside. If your dough has bubbled up in the bottom, use the back of a spoon to gently push it back down, making sure to get into the corners and up the sides.

4   While the shell is baking, make the hazelnut praliné. Place the hazelnuts on a baking sheet and toast in the oven for 10 minutes. Straight from the oven pour them into a clean tea towel and close it up like a sack. Rub the nuts together in the towel to remove the husks. It's OK if you can't get all of them off.

5   Line a baking sheet with parchment paper. In a small pot, add the sugar and cook over medium-high to make a caramel. When the edges start to liquify and brown, use a spatula to push it upward toward the center and gently stir until honey-colored, 2 minutes. Do not walk away during this step—it will happen so fast. Err on the lighter side for the caramelization so it doesn't become bitter. Add the salt and toasted hazelnuts and stir to coat. Pour the mixture out onto the prepared baking sheet in a flat layer to cool.

6   Break up the nutty caramel into small shards and add to the bowl of a food processor. Process on high

cont'd

speed until it turns into a paste, scraping down the bowl as necessary, 5 minutes.

7   Transfer the praliné to the blind-baked tart shell and spread it into a thin, even layer.

8   To make the custard filling, in a medium mixing bowl, combine the **eggs**, **egg yolks**, **cornstarch**, **vanilla**, and **salt**. Whisk by hand until pale and fluffy, about 1 minute.

9   In a medium saucepan, combine the **milk**, **cream**, and **sugar**. Bring to a scald—small bubbles around the edges, right before boiling—over medium-high heat. Slowly pour the hot milk into the egg mixture, whisking constantly to prevent the eggs from scrambling.

10 Return the mixture to the pot over medium-high heat and continue to whisk until it starts to boil and thicken, about 2 minutes. Pour the custard into the tart shell and bake on the top rack of the oven until set but still jiggly in the center, 20 minutes. Sprinkle the 1 Tbsp of **sugar** over the top of the custard and place it back in the oven on broil until caramelized spots appear, 2 to 3 minutes. Keep a close eye on this part, as it can burn very quickly. Allow to cool completely before transferring to the refrigerator to chill for 6 hours or overnight. Unmold, slice, and serve.

Pro Tips & Storage

- The tart can be stored in an airtight container or covered in plastic wrap for up to 3 days in the refrigerator.

- The hazelnut praliné can be stored in a jar or airtight container for up to 2 weeks in the refrigerator. This is also a great spread on toast.

- Try swapping out the hazelnut praliné for shredded coconut, sliced fresh bananas, mangoes, or other fruit.

Vietnamese Coffee Viennetta

Growing up, I never knew Viennettas were popular in the States, since the only time I ever enjoyed one was when my family and I traveled to Hong Kong to visit my grandparents. My grandmother always bought one as a special treat for me and my sister. Presumably due to the British influence in Hong Kong, Viennetta ice cream cakes were a prized possession to be shared with family. I will forever associate this magical frozen treat with memories of my grandmother.

Here, I combine a Viennetta with a classic Carvel ice cream cake by filling it with crunchies. I call mine "cronchies" because that's how my team of cooks would label them. They provide the perfect crunch in between layers of condensed milk ice cream, fudge, and Vietnamese coffee ice cream.

YIELD: Makes 6 to 8 servings

ICE CREAMS

1 recipe Condensed Milk Ice Cream (page 166)

1 packet instant Vietnamese coffee or 1 Tbsp regular instant coffee

HOT FUDGE

¼ cup + 3 Tbsp [95 g] dark brown sugar

⅓ cup [80 ml] heavy cream

4 Tbsp [55 g] unsalted butter, cut into chunks

¼ cup [30 g] Dutch-process cocoa powder

1 tsp vanilla extract

¼ tsp kosher salt

PÂTE À GLACER & CRONCHIES

¼ cup [40 g] semisweet (60% cacao) chocolate chunks

1 tsp coconut oil

2 sugar cones or 1 waffle cone

Pinch kosher salt

1 Line the inside of an 8 by 4 by 4 in [20 by 10 by 10 cm] Pullman pan or standard loaf pan with parchment or wax paper. An easy way to do it is to cut two strips of paper: one strip the width of the pan and wide enough to go up the sides, and another strip the length of the pan and long enough to go up the ends. Place one strip on top of the other like a cross and place it in the loaf pan appropriately.

2 To make the ice creams, make the condensed milk ice cream, steps 5 and 6, but leave it in the mixer bowl. Transfer 2 cups [300 g] of the ice cream base to the loaf pan and smooth it out. Give it a couple light taps on the counter to make sure it settles flat and into the corners, then place it in the freezer to set for 1 hour.

3 Transfer another 2 cups [300 g] of the ice cream base to a mixing bowl and add the instant coffee. Whisk by hand until dissolved. Cover the bowl with plastic wrap and place it in the refrigerator. Transfer the remaining base to a piping bag fitted with a decorative tip (for the classic look, use a ½ in [13 mm] ribbon tip) and place in the refrigerator.

4 To make the hot fudge, in a medium saucepan, combine the brown sugar, cream, butter, and cocoa powder and cook over medium-high heat, whisking together as it melts. Once everything is dissolved and smooth, add the vanilla and salt and whisk to combine. Transfer to a jar or airtight container and allow to cool at room temperature. For this cake, use the fudge while it's barely warm and not scorching hot.

5 To make the pâte à glacer, melt the chocolate over a double boiler or in the microwave in 30 second increments, stirring in between. Add the coconut oil and whisk until smooth.

6 To make the cronchies, in a medium mixing bowl crush the cones by hand into small fragments the size of a cat treat. Pour over the pâte à glacer. Mix with a spoon, making sure all the cone pieces are covered. Scrape it out onto a parchment-lined plate or baking sheet. Spread it out into a thin layer

cont'd

and place in the freezer for 20 minutes. Break up the cronchies into smaller shards into the bowl of a food processor. Pulse until it forms little balls of crunchy chocolatey-ness. Spread the cronchies back out onto the parchment-lined baking sheet and keep in the freezer until ready to use.

7   Remove the loaf pan from the freezer and sprinkle a generous ¼ in [6 mm] thick layer of cronchies over the condensed milk ice cream. Reserve 1 Tbsp of the cronchies for garnish. Pour a ¼ in [6 mm] thick layer of fudge over the cronchies. Use the back of a spoon or small offset spatula to spread the fudge into an even layer. Return to the freezer for 30 minutes. Reserve at least ¼ cup of the fudge for garnish.

8   Remove the loaf pan from the freezer and spread the reserved coffee ice cream over the top of the fudge. Give it a couple gentle taps again to help it settle into an even layer. Place in the freezer for at least 4 hours or, better, overnight.

And yes, it will be OK to keep the base in the piping bag in the fridge overnight.

9   Place a serving platter on top of the loaf pan and flip to unmold the cake. You may have to carefully run the sides of the pan under warm water if it doesn't pop out. Obviously, do not get water inside the cake. Peel off the parchment paper.

10   Remove the chilled piping bag with the reserved condensed milk ice cream from the refrigerator. If the base has become too loose to hold its shape, you can quickly rewhip it until stiff again. Pipe ribbons of the fluffy ice cream base in a decorative manner on the top of the cake. If you have enough, you can also pipe around the base of the cake. Place it in the freezer to set for 1 hour.

11   Drizzle the top of the ribbons with more hot fudge or pâte à glacer. You will likely need to warm either of them up to turn it back to a liquid state. Heat in the microwave at

10 second increments, stirring in between until smooth. Garnish the top with more cronchies, slice, and serve.

Pro Tips & Storage

- The Viennetta can be stored in an airtight container or wrapped in plastic wrap for up to 3 months in the freezer.
- The hot fudge can be stored in a jar or airtight container for up to 2 weeks in the refrigerator.
- The pâte à glacer can be stored in an airtight container for up to 3 weeks in the refrigerator.
- The cronchies can be stored in an airtight container for up to 3 months in the freezer (freeze in a single layer first).
- The pâte à glacer can be used to dip strawberries or as a chocolate coating for anything.

Thai Tea Gelati

The term "gelati" in this case refers to the Italian American dessert that can be found most often in New York: Italian ice spots that serve a parfait of alternating layers of ice cream or soft serve with Italian ice. I love the contrast in textures between the smooth and creamy ice cream and the icy crystals of Italian ice, slush, or granita.

This is probably the easiest recipe in this book (and, dare I say, possibly the yummiest). Each bite you take leaves you wanting more. It is refreshing and sweet with the perfect tang. Of course, if you are not a fan of Thai tea, then you are SOL on this one, but you should make the condensed milk ice cream anyway because yum, and it's a great base for other flavors (see Pro Tips).

YIELD: Makes 3 quarts

THAI ICED TEA GRANITA

¾ cup [75 g] Thai tea leaves mix

½ cup [100 g] granulated sugar

¼ cup [60 ml] lemon juice

CONDENSED MILK ICE CREAM

2 cups [480 ml] heavy cream, cold

One 14 oz [415 ml] can sweetened condensed milk

¼ tsp kosher salt

BROWN SUGAR BOBA (OPTIONAL)

1 cup [140 g] large black boba pearls

1 cup [200 g] dark brown sugar

1   To make the Thai tea granita, in a medium saucepan, bring 3 cups [720 ml] of water to a boil. Remove from the heat and add the tea leaves, stir, and let it steep for 10 minutes.

2   Strain the tea through a fine-mesh sieve into a 2-quart freezer-proof airtight container, using the back of a spoon to press all the liquid out of the leaves. Discard the tea leaves.

3   Add the sugar and lemon juice to the tea and whisk until the sugar is completely dissolved. Cover and place in the freezer for 3 hours.

4   Use a fork to scrape the top layer of ice crystals like shaved ice. Ideally you will place it back in the freezer for another 3 hours and repeat until the tea is completely frozen and you're left with a pile of fluffy granita. But if you don't have time to sit there all day and stare at your granita, just scrape it when you can.

5   To make the condensed milk ice cream, in the bowl of a stand mixer fitted with the whisk attachment, whip the cream until it just reaches stiff peaks. Do not overwhip.

6   With the mixer running on medium-low speed, drizzle in the condensed milk and add the salt. Whip until fully combined. The base should still be very fluffy and not deflated. Transfer to a freezer-proof airtight container and freeze for at least 6 hours.

7   If not using the boba, skip this step. Cook the boba according to the package instructions and drain. In a medium saucepan, bring the brown sugar and 1 cup [240 ml] of water to a boil. Continue to simmer until thickened into a syrup, about 10 minutes. Add the cooked boba and stir.

8   Gather rocks glasses or bowls to serve. Place a scoop of condensed milk ice cream at the bottom of the glass. Top with some granita, add another scoop of ice cream and some more granita, and finish with a couple spoonfuls of boba. Repeat for as many servings as you need.

cont'd

Pro Tips & Storage

- The ice cream and granita will stay fresh for up to 3 months in the freezer. The boba can be stored in the syrup in an airtight container for up to 1 week in the refrigerator.

- Scraping the granita every few hours is the best way to keep uniform crystals and flavor, but if you don't have time to do this every few hours, just scrape it when you can. Even if you leave it to freeze in a solid block overnight, it will still work.

- You can turn this ice cream into a multitude of flavors to eat on its own. Try folding in cookie pieces, candy, or fresh fruit after whipping.

- Make a sundae using this ice cream recipe with Hot Fudge (page 163) or pour over Pâte à Glacer (page 163) as a magic shell.

Ovaltine Mochi Marjolaine

One of my favorite desserts I learned in culinary school is called a marjolaine, a French seven-layer cake comprised of layers of nutty meringues, ganaches, and buttercreams. Growing up, I loved Ovaltine, a chocolate malted milk powder similar to hot chocolate mix. Though it originates from the United Kingdom, it is popular all over Asia due to British colonization and influence.

Marjolaines are naturally gluten-free, so I thought, why not add layers of mochi cake to the mix for an extra textural element? This dessert has the most steps out of all recipes included in this book, but the result is a rich, decadent, chewy, and nutty total stunner of a cake that is well worth the effort.

Make sure to read through all the recipes and have all your components ready before assembling.

YIELD: Makes 8 to 10 servings

Chocolate Mochi Cake (recipe follows)
Almond Dacquoise (recipe follow)
Ovaltine Ganache (recipe follows)
Stabilized Malted Chantilly (recipe follows)
8 recipes Pâte à Glacer (page 163)
¾ cup [18 g] Rice Krispies cereal
Ovaltine Buttercream (recipe follows)

1 Make sure to have all the components ready before assembling.

2 Remove the **mochi cake** and **dacquoise** from the freezer. Take them out of the pans and peel off the parchments. Place the mochi cake on a clean piece of parchment paper. The paper should be bigger than the cake so you can easily pick it up by the edges of the parchment. Spread the **Ovaltine ganache** on top in an even layer.

3 Place the dacquoise layer on top of the ganache and gently press down to stick. Spread a ½ in [13 mm] thick layer of **malted Chantilly** over the dacquoise, then place the entire cake in the freezer for 30 minutes to chill.

4 Meanwhile, make the **pâte à glacer**. When it's warm, not hot, but still liquid, stir in the **Rice Krispies**. Set aside while you finish assembling the cake.

5 Take the cake out of the freezer and, using a ruler, cut the cake in half lengthwise, yielding two 4 by 12 in [10 by 30 cm] pieces of cake. Spread the Chantilly on top of one half, then place the other half on top and transfer it to a cutting board. Using a serrated cake or bread knife, trim off about ½ in [13 mm] from each side. Don't worry so much about the measurement; the goal is to just get straight edges on each side of the cake, forming an even rectangle.

6 Coat the cake in a thin layer of **Ovaltine buttercream** and smooth out the edges and corners with an offset spatula or cake scraper. Place in the refrigerator to set for about 10 minutes.

7 Apply a second coat of buttercream and smooth it out. It should be about ¼ in [6 mm] thick, and you shouldn't be able to see any cake peeking through. Try to get the edges as smooth and straight as possible. Place back in the refrigerator for 10 minutes. Reserve the rest of the buttercream to decorate the top.

8 Line a 13 by 17 in [33 by 43 cm] baking sheet with parchment paper and place a wire rack on top. Gently remove the parchment paper from under the cake and place the cake directly on top of the wire rack.

cont'd

9 Check the prepared pâte à glacer. If it has set up too much, micro-wave in 10 second increments until it is warm, but not hot. Working quickly and with intention, pour the glaze over the top of the cake, allowing it to drip down and cover the sides. It should set up pretty quickly.

10 Carefully slide an offset spatula under the cake to loosen and trans-fer it back to the serving platter.

11 Prepare a piping bag with a large St. Honoré piping tip (Ateco 883; see Pro Tips if you don't have one) and fill it with the leftover butter-cream. Pipe random squiggles in a decorative manner on top of the glazed cake to finish.

cont'd

Chocolate Mochi Cake

2 cups [220 g] Mochiko or glutinous rice flour

1¼ cups [250 g] granulated sugar

2½ Tbsp Dutch-process cocoa powder, sifted

1½ tsp baking soda

½ tsp kosher salt

¾ cup [180 ml] full-fat coconut milk

½ cup [120 ml] evaporated milk

2 large eggs

3 Tbsp unsalted butter, melted

1 tsp vanilla extract

1 Preheat the oven to 375°F [190°C]. Grease a 9 by 13 in [23 by 33 cm] quarter baking sheet with nonstick spray or butter and line with parchment paper.

2 In a large mixing bowl, combine the Mochiko, sugar, cocoa powder, baking soda, and salt. Whisk to combine.

3 In medium mixing bowl, whisk together the coconut milk, evaporated milk, eggs, butter, and vanilla.

4 Pour the wet ingredients into the bowl of dry ingredients and whisk until combined and smooth and there are no lumps.

5 Pour the batter into the prepared baking sheet and bake until cooked through and the cake springs back to the touch, 40 to 45 minutes.

6 Allow the cake to cool in the pan for 1 hour before placing it in the freezer to chill for at least 2 hours.

Almond Dacquoise

7 large egg whites
¼ tsp kosher salt
¼ tsp cream of tartar (optional)
1 cup [200 g] granulated sugar
1⅔ cups [200 g] almond flour

1   Preheat the oven to 250°F [120°C]. Grease only the bottom, not the sides, of a 9 by 13 in [23 by 33 cm] quarter baking sheet with nonstick spray or butter. Line just the bottom of the baking sheet with parchment paper.

2   In the bowl of a stand mixer fitted with the whisk attachment, whisk the egg whites, salt, and cream of tartar, if using, on medium-high speed.

3   When the egg whites start to get foamy, add the sugar in three additions, whisking for about 30 seconds in between each. Continue to whisk on high speed until stiff peaks form. The meringue should be smooth and glossy and still have some flexibility. Do not overwhip.

4   Sift the almond flour into a large mixing bowl. Add about one third of the meringue and fold it in using a rubber spatula until incorporated like a paste. Then fold in the rest of the meringue until combined and no streaks remain, trying to use as few strokes as possible to avoid deflating the meringue.

5   Transfer the dacquoise batter to the prepared baking sheet and, using an offset spatula, smooth it out to the edges in an even layer. Bake until very lightly browned around the edges and cooked all the way through, 45 to 50 minutes.

6   Allow the dacquoise to cool in the pan for 1 hour before placing it in the freezer to chill for at least 2 hours.

cont'd

Ovaltine Ganache

⅔ cup [100 g] milk chocolate pistoles or chunks

¼ cup + 2 Tbsp [90 ml] heavy cream

1½ Tbsp Ovaltine

1 Tbsp unsalted butter, at room temperature

1   Place the **chocolate** in a medium mixing bowl. In a small pot, heat the **heavy cream** to a scald—small bubbles around the edges, right before boiling. Pour the heavy cream over the chocolate and let it sit for 1 minute to soften.

2   Add the **Ovaltine** and whisk until smooth. Whisk in the **butter**. Use a stick blender on low speed to finish emulsifying the ganache. If you don't have a stick blender, use a regular blender on the lowest setting. Process until smooth and shiny, about 30 seconds.

3   Place a piece of plastic wrap directly touching the top of the ganache and let sit at room temperature for about 2 hours until thickened.

Stabilized Malted Chantilly

1 cup [240 ml] heavy cream

3 Tbsp powdered sugar

3 Tbsp malted milk powder

¼ tsp kosher salt

¾ tsp powdered gelatin

1   This should be made when you are ready to assemble your cake and used immediately. In the bowl of a stand mixer fitted with the whisk attachment, add the **heavy cream**, **powdered sugar**, **malted milk powder**, and **salt**. Whip on medium-high speed until it forms medium peaks.

2   Meanwhile, place 1 Tbsp of water in a small dish and sprinkle the **gelatin** over the top. Allow it to sit and bloom, about 2 minutes. Place it in the microwave for about 7 seconds to melt. Set aside.

3   With the mixer running, pour the melted gelatin into the cream and continue to whip until it forms stiff peaks. Do not overwhip.

cont'd

Ovaltine Buttercream

1½ cups [300 g] granulated sugar

5 large egg whites

¼ tsp kosher salt

1 lb [455 g] unsalted butter, cubed, at room temperature

¾ cup [75 g] Ovaltine

⅔ cup [100 g] semisweet chocolate chunks, barely melted and not too hot

2 tsp vanilla extract

1 In a small saucepan, stir together the **sugar** and ½ cup [120 ml] of water. Bring to a boil over medium-high heat and continue to cook until it reaches 238°F [115°C].

2 Meanwhile, in the bowl of a stand mixer fitted with the whisk attachment, whip the **egg whites** and **salt** together until it forms medium peaks.

3 When the sugar is ready, and with the stand mixer on medium speed, slowly drizzle in the sugar syrup down the side of the bowl. Continue to whip on medium-high speed until the bowl is barely warm to the touch, 5 to 10 minutes.

4 Add the **butter** several cubes at a time, allowing the mixture to come back together before adding more. Once all the butter is in, add the **Ovaltine** and mix until incorporated. By now it should look like a beautiful silky buttercream. (See Pro Tips for troubleshooting.)

5 With the stand mixer running on medium speed, slowly drizzle in the melted **chocolate** and **vanilla**. Continue to whisk until smooth, silky, and fluffy, 1 to 2 minutes more.

6 Transfer to an airtight container and set aside at room temperature until ready to use.

Pro Tips & Storage

- The marjolaine is best served at room temperature or slightly chilled.
- The completed marjolaine can be kept in an airtight container for up to 1 week in the refrigerator or 3 months in the freezer.
- Both the mochi cake and dacquoise can be made in advance and frozen for up to 3 months.
- The ganache can be made in advance and kept in an airtight container for up to 1 week in the refrigerator. Bring it back to room temperature and stir before using.
- The buttercream can be made in advance and kept in an airtight container for up to 1 week in the refrigerator or 3 months in the freezer. In either case, the buttercream should be brought to room temperature and paddled in a stand mixer until smooth before using.

- This is a great basic ganache recipe. You can leave out the Ovaltine, swap out the milk chocolate for semisweet or white, and use it in any application that calls for a ganache.
- This is a great Italian meringue buttercream recipe. You can leave out the Ovaltine for a chocolate buttercream, or leave out both and add vanilla bean, powder, or extract for a vanilla buttercream.
- Leave out the malted milk powder and add 1 tsp of vanilla extract for a regular stabilized whipped cream.
- You can leave the gelatin out of the whipped cream, but the final cake may not last as long and could become misshapen.
- Feeling lazy but want something rich and chocolatey? Try baking the Chocolate Mochi Cake in an 8 in [20 cm] square pan and frosting the top with a triple recipe of Ovaltine Ganache.

- If you don't have a St. Honoré piping tip, here's an easy hack: Take a disposable piping bag and cut the tip off, leaving ½ in [13 mm] wide opening. With the piping bag still folded in half, mark a dot ⅛ in [3 mm] inward from the opening you just cut. Mark a dot 1 in [2.5 cm] up the side of the piping bag. Connect the two dots and cut along that line.

SNACKS

I come from a family of proud snackers. One time (maybe multiple times), my dad went to the airport with an entire suitcase filled with his favorite Costco snacks to bring to his friends and family in China, but alas, it weighed well over the limit of 50 pounds. Instead of paying the extra fee, or removing some of Costco's finest, he and my mom devised the ingenious idea to leave the entire suitcase behind in Los Angeles for my mother to divvy up between a carry-on and checked bag, which she would later bring with her after purchasing her own flight to Hong Kong where my father would meet her to collect his goods.

This is not a joke. My mom literally bought an entire roundtrip trans-Pacific flight just to meet my dad in Hong Kong to deliver to him his Costco treats and return with a whole suitcase filled with her own favorite snacks from Hong Kong.

This chapter is an ode to all those times my parents came home with cases of magnificent munchies from around the world for me and my sister to try. From one snacker to another, here is a trove of smaller bites, from savory snacks to cookies and confections, that will cure your hankering for that little something.

Chee Cheung Fun
Plain Rice Noodle Rolls

One of my favorite snacks are the chee cheung fun (rice noodle rolls) from a small stall just outside of the Star Ferry on the Hong Kong side. Every visit to Hong Kong came with plenty of back and forth on this ferry. The backs of the seats were all connected on a swivel so they could easily be switched to face whichever direction you were going. Once everyone got out of their seats, my sister and I would go up and down the aisles reorienting the seats to be neatly facing forward.

Before getting on the ferry, we always had to stop at a small window located outside the entrance, where they served curry fish balls and a pile of rice rolls in a paper bag, smothered with all the sauces. We looked forward to this part the most and could never get enough. I developed my own recipe for rice rolls so I can share this memory with you.

YIELD: Makes thirteen 9 in [23 cm] rolls

1¼ cups [140 g] rice flour

⅓ cup + 1 Tbsp [50 g] tapioca flour

2 Tbsp wheat starch

1 Tbsp vegetable oil

2 tsp granulated sugar

½ tsp kosher salt

TO SERVE (OPTIONAL)

Soy sauce

Hoisin sauce

Peanut sauce

Sriracha

Scallions, finely chopped

Sesame seeds

1   To make the batter, in a medium mixing bowl, whisk together 2½ cups [600 ml] of water, the **rice flour, tapioca flour, wheat starch, vegetable oil, sugar,** and **salt** until combined.

2   Set up a steamer with one basket. Place a flat tray, plate, or pan inside the steamer basket and bring the water to a boil. Ideally you will use a rimmed tray, but my bamboo steamer is not big enough, so I put a 9 in [23 cm] cake pan inside. Find something that works for you.

3   Grease the inside of the pan with nonstick spray or vegetable oil. Pour ¼ cup [60 ml] of the batter into the pan and tilt and swirl to get an even layer. Cover and lower the heat to keep it at a simmer. Steam until translucent, 2 to 3 minutes.

4   Using the flat edge of a rubber spatula, gently lift up one edge of the rice roll and roll it away from you into a log. Transfer to a cutting board and repeat with the rest; you will do this 10 to 13 more times,

depending on the size of your steamer and pan. Add more water to the steamer as necessary. Make sure to regrease the pan each time and stir the batter frequently, as it will separate.

5   Cut the rice rolls into 2 in [5 cm] segments and top with **soy sauce, hoisin sauce, peanut sauce, sriracha, scallions,** and **sesame seeds,** if desired.

Pro Tips & Storage

- Leftover rice rolls can be stored in an airtight container for up to 3 days in the refrigerator.

- This is a great rice roll recipe. You can use it in any application that calls for fresh rice noodles by cutting the flat sheets into strips instead of rolling them up.

- Try placing some shrimp, Char Siu Carnitas (page 40), Hong Kong Bolognese (page 51), Chinese Bacon, Egg & Chive Filling (page 57), or Wild Mushroom–Boursin Filling without the cheese (page 65) on top while steaming, before rolling it up.

Ramen Cheese Itz

When I had my own business in Brooklyn, my sous chef Lauren used to always talk about eating her instant ramen with cheese on top. At that time, I was taken aback and asked what the hell she was talking about, to which she replied with a tone of shock at my ignorance, "Yeah, man, it's so freaking good!"

Since then I feel like all I see is cheese on ramen. In Korea, it's so commonplace that you will even find cheddar-flavored instant noodles. In some Asian markets you can find ramen snacks that are basically broken up pieces of dried ramen covered in various flavor dusts and packaged like a bag of potato chips. For this recipe I wanted to create a cheesy ramen snack, so I combined that idea with one of my favorite American snacks: the Cheez-It. And like Lauren said, man, it's so freaking good.

YIELD: Makes about two hundred 1 in [2.5 cm] square crackers

One 2 oz [55 g] pack uncooked ramen

4 oz [115 g] sharp cheddar cheese, shredded (about 1½ cups)

1 cup [150 g] all-purpose flour

¾ cup [170 g] unsalted butter, cubed, cold

1 Tbsp chicken bouillon

1 tsp white miso

½ tsp garlic powder

½ tsp ichimi togarashi or ground cayenne pepper

¼ cup [60 ml] cold water

1 In the bowl of a food processor, pulse the **ramen** until it becomes a fine powder. You can use a mortar and pestle or spice grinder to finish the job if necessary. Since not all ramen packs weigh the same, measure out ⅓ cup [55 g] of the dust (if you have extra, discard the rest). Return the dust to the food processor and add the **cheese** and **flour** and process until it resembles a coarse meal, about 30 seconds. Add the **butter, chicken bouillon, miso, garlic powder,** and **togarashi** and process until the butter chunks are the size of lentils. With the machine running, slowly pour in the **water** until the dough just comes together. The dough will be very sticky.

2 Divide the dough in half and place one portion in between two pieces of parchment paper roughly measuring 12 by 16 in [30.5 by 40.5 cm]. Roll it out to ⅛ in [3 mm] thick, mimicking the shape of the parchment. Place the dough on a baking sheet and put in the freezer to chill for 30 minutes. If it doesn't fit flat in your freezer, place it in the refrigerator. Repeat with the other portion of dough.

3 Preheat the oven to 350°F [180°C]. Line three 13 by 17 in [33 by 43 cm] baking sheets with parchment paper and set aside. Working with one sheet of dough at a time, peel off one side of parchment, gently lay it back on the dough, flip, and peel the other side off.

cont'd

4   Use a knife or ravioli cutter to cut
a grid of 1 in [2.5 cm] squares in
the dough. Transfer each square
to a prepared baking sheet ¼ in
[6 mm] apart. Repeat with the other
sheet of dough. Gather the scraps
together and reroll them once more
to get more crackers. I like to turn
my reroll scraps into one giant
cracker because it's hilarious. Try to
work quickly; if the dough becomes
too soft to transfer the pieces to the
baking sheet, throw it back in the
fridge or freezer for a few minutes
to firm up.

5   Use a chopstick or the blunt end of
a skewer to poke a hole in the center of each cracker. Bake the crackers, in batches if necessary, until
crisp and slightly darker around the
edges, 15 to 18 minutes. Allow to
cool on the baking sheets.

Pro Tips & Storage

- The baked crackers can be kept in an airtight container for up to 4 days at room temperature.

- The dough can be made in advance and kept wrapped in plastic wrap or between parchment paper for up to 2 days in the refrigerator or 3 months in the freezer.

- The dough is pretty sticky, so freezing the sheets flat is the easiest way to get clean cuts and perfectly square crackers. If it doesn't fit in the freezer you can refrigerate it, but keep in mind it may be harder to work with. You may have to work faster with a little more finesse.

- I always have packs of plain ramen noodles in the house. If you have the individual packs that come with a sea-soning packet and you love that fla-vor, feel free to substitute that packet for the seasonings in the recipe.

Ginger-Togarashi Cookies with Lemon Icing

If you've ever visited New York City during the holiday season, you may have gone to the winter village at Bryant Park. Every year they turn the park into an ice rink surrounded by food and gift kiosks in the shape of cute little glass houses. It really is quite magical, but for all the people working those kiosks, it's not very fun. I know because I used to have one there every winter with my old business, The Baking Bean.

One of our signature seasonal treats was a gingerbread man cookie sandwich filled with lemon icing. It's become the favorite cookie I've ever made, and not just during the holidays. Here I have cut them out into pretzels because the color is appropriate. The inclusion of togarashi, a Japanese chili spice blend, adds the perfect kick and subtle savory notes.

YIELD: Makes 10 sandwich cookies

LEMON ICING

2 cups [240 g] powdered sugar

6 Tbsp [85 g] unsalted butter, melted

1 lemon, zest + 2 Tbsp juice

1 tsp shichimi togarashi

GINGERBREAD-TOGARASHI COOKIES

6 Tbsp [85 g] unsalted butter, at room temperature

¼ cup + 3 Tbsp [95 g] dark brown sugar

1 large egg

1 Tbsp molasses

½ orange, zest + 1 tsp juice

1½ cups + 1 Tbsp [220 g] all-purpose flour

1 tsp ground cinnamon

1 tsp ground ginger

½ tsp baking soda

½ tsp shichimi togarashi

¼ tsp ground cloves

¼ tsp kosher salt

2 Tbsp crystal sugar (optional)

1 To make the lemon icing, in a medium mixing bowl, combine the powdered sugar, butter, lemon zest, lemon juice, and togarashi. Stir until smooth and no lumps remain. Place a piece of plastic wrap directly touching the surface and place in the refrigerator for 1 hour to chill.

2 To make the gingerbread-togarashi cookies, in the bowl of a stand mixer fitted with the paddle attachment, cream together the butter and brown sugar on medium speed until light and fluffy, about 2 minutes. Meanwhile, in a liquid measuring cup, add the egg, molasses, orange zest, and orange juice and whisk to combine.

3 Scrape down the sides of the mixer bowl and, with the mixer running, stream in the egg mixture in four additions, allowing it to combine before adding the next. Scrape down the bowl as needed and continue to paddle until smooth.

4 Scrape down the bowl again and add the flour, cinnamon, ginger, baking soda, togarashi, cloves, and salt. Mix on medium-low speed until it comes together into a smooth dough, 1 to 2 minutes.

5 Divide the dough in half and place one portion in between two pieces of parchment paper roughly measuring 12 by 16 in [30.5 by 40.5 cm]. Roll it out to ⅛ in [3 mm] thick, mimicking the shape of the parchment. Place the dough on a baking sheet and put it in the refrigerator to chill for 30 minutes. Repeat with the other portion of dough.

6 Preheat the oven to 350°F [180°C]. Working with one baking sheet at a time, peel off one side of parchment, gently lay it back on the dough, flip, and peel the other side off. I used a 2½ in [6 cm] wide pretzel-shaped cookie cutter, but you can use whatever shape you like. Place the cut cookies onto a parchment-lined baking sheet. Repeat with the other sheet of dough. Gather the scraps together

cont'd

and reroll them once more to get more cookies.

7   Sprinkle the **crystal sugar**, if using, over the tops of half the cookies. Bake until the edges are slightly darker, 10 to 12 minutes. Allow to cool on the baking sheets or wire racks.

8   Check on the lemon icing and give it a stir. You want it to be soft enough to retain its shape when piped. Transfer the icing to a disposable piping bag and cut a ¼ in [6 mm] opening at the tip. Flip over the half of the cookies that have not been topped with crystal sugar. Pipe the lemon icing on the flat side of the cookies and place the other half of the cookies over the icing to form a cookie sandwich.

9   You can eat them straight away, but the icing will probably ooze out. It is best to allow the cookies to sit out at room temperature, uncovered, for at least 4 hours so the icing can set and become firm.

Pro Tips & Storage

- The fully assembled cookie sandwiches can be stored in airtight containers for up to 1 week at room temperature.

- The cookie dough can be made in advance and stored, wrapped in plastic wrap or rolled between parchment paper, for up to 2 days in the refrigerator or 3 months in the freezer.

- The icing can be made in advance and stored in an airtight container for up to 4 days in the refrigerator. It will need to be brought to room temperature before piping.

- This is a great cookie for decorating with royal icing, especially during the holidays. Use a gingerbread man cookie cutter and skip the lemon icing for plain gingerbread cookies.

- The amount of icing in the recipe is good enough for 3 in [8 cm] circle cookies. If you happen to use a pretzel cutter, you will only need a half recipe of lemon icing.

Matcha Shortbread with Raspberry Ganache

I went through a phase in my late teens where I was obsessed with Walker's shortbread cookies. I loved the crumbly layers of lightly caramelized butter and sugar, so rich and filling—yet I could down a whole box in one sitting, no sweat.

One of our signature treats at The Baking Bean was a raspberry shortbread cookie sandwich filled with matcha ganache. For this book I wanted to try and flip the script and make the matcha on the outside and raspberry on the inside. The result is so good; the sweet tang from the raspberry ganache melts in your mouth alongside caramelized butter and nutty notes from the matcha. I could easily down a whole batch of these in one sitting, but I think my stomach might punch me for it later.

YIELD: Makes ten 1½ in [4 cm] sandwich cookies

RASPBERRY GANACHE

1 cup [120 g] raspberries, fresh or frozen, thawed

⅓ cup [65 g] granulated sugar

¾ tsp citric acid or juice of 1 lemon

2 Tbsp heavy cream

1 Tbsp cornstarch

½ cup [75 g] white chocolate chunks

5 Tbsp [70 g] unsalted butter, cubed and at room temperature

¼ tsp kosher salt

MATCHA SHORTBREAD

½ cup [113 g] unsalted butter, at room temperature

¼ cup [50 g] granulated sugar

1 cup + 2 Tbsp [160 g] all-purpose flour

1 tsp ceremonial-grade matcha

Pinch kosher salt

1   To make the raspberry ganache, in a blender, purée the **raspberries**. Strain through a fine-mesh sieve into a small saucepan, using the back of a spoon to push out as much liquid as possible. Whisk in the **sugar** and **citric acid**. Bring to a boil over medium-high heat.

2   Meanwhile, in a small dish, whisk together the **cream** and **cornstarch**. Add this mixture to the saucepan once the raspberry mixture has come to a boil. Whisk continually until thickened, about 2 minutes.

3   Place the **white chocolate** in a mixing bowl and pour over the thickened raspberry mixture. Allow to sit for 1 minute, then whisk to combine. Add the **butter** and **salt** and whisk to incorporate. Use a stick blender (or a regular blender on low speed) to finish emulsifying the ganache until velvety smooth. Place a piece of plastic wrap directly touching the surface of the ganache and place in the refrigerator for 1 hour to chill.

4   To make the matcha shortbread, in the bowl of a stand mixer fitted with the paddle attachment, cream together the **butter** and **sugar** on medium speed until light and fluffy, about 2 minutes.

5   Scrape down the sides of the bowl and add the **flour**, **matcha**, and **salt**.

Paddle on medium-low speed until just combined. Depending on the size of your mixer bowl, it may look more like a pebbly streusel dough. As long as the dough sticks when clumped together, it's fine.

6   Divide the dough in half and place one portion in between two pieces of parchment paper roughly measuring 12 by 16 in [30.5 by 40.5 cm]. Roll it out to ⅛ in [3 mm] thick, mimicking the shape of the parchment. Place on a baking sheet and put it in the refrigerator to chill for 30 minutes. Repeat with the other portion of dough.

7   Preheat the oven to 350°F [180°C]. Working with one baking sheet at a time, peel off one side of parchment, gently lay it back on the dough, flip, and peel the other side off. I used a mooncake press to stamp designs all over the dough, then a 1½ in [4 cm] circle cutter to cut them out. If you don't have a mooncake press, you can just use the circle cutter or any other cookie cutter shape you wish. Place the

cont'd

cut cookies onto a parchment-lined baking sheet. Repeat with the other sheet of dough. Gather the scraps together and reroll them once more to get more cookies.

8 Bake the cookies until lightly golden brown around the edges, 12 to 15 minutes. Allow to cool on the baking sheets or wire racks.

9 Check on the ganache; you want it to be the consistency of soft butter so you can pipe it. Give it a stir until smooth. If it's too loose, allow it to chill more until you get the desired consistency. Transfer the ganache to a piping bag and cut a ¼ in [6 mm] opening at the tip. Grab a cookie and flip it over, pipe a spiral of ganache, and top with another cookie, gently pressing so the ganache fills out to the edges. You can eat them straight away, but the ganache will probably ooze out. It is best to allow the cookies to sit out at room temperature, uncovered, for at least 6 hours so the ganache can set and become firm.

Pro Tips & Storage

- The fully assembled cookie sandwiches can be stored in airtight containers for up to 4 days at room temperature or 1 week in the refrigerator.

- The cookie dough can be made in advance and stored, wrapped in plastic wrap or rolled between parchment paper, for up to 2 days in the refrigerator or 3 months in the freezer.

- The ganache can be made in advance and stored in an airtight container for up to 4 days in the refrigerator.

- Try swapping the filling out for Lemon Icing (page 185).

- Try swapping out the raspberries for another berry.

- If you want to make just the cookies, roll the dough out thicker, to ¼ in [6 mm]. Cut them into squares or rectangles and top with sanding or crystal sugar before baking.

- If you want a plain shortbread, simply eliminate the matcha powder and add the seeds from a vanilla bean or 1 tsp of vanilla extract.

Digestive Cookies with Horlicks Ganache

Horlicks is a warm malted-milk drink that is popular in the United Kingdom and other Commonwealth countries, which at one time included Hong Kong, where I learned to love it. My mom would take trips to Hong Kong without us, but she always brought back the latest in Horlicks-inspired treats. Our favorite was in the form of a dime-sized candy tablet that dissolved in your mouth.

Another United Kingdom favorite of mine is the digestive biscuit, a thin semisweet whole-wheat cookie that is often eaten with tea or coffee. I especially love the ones that have a thin coating of milk chocolate on the top. To me Horlicks and digestives go together like bread and butter, so I just reimagined one of those malted candy tablets sandwiched between two inverted chocolate-coated digestives, and this is how it turned out.

YIELD: Makes fifteen 2 in [5 cm] sandwich cookies

HORLICKS GANACHE

½ cup [75 g] milk chocolate chunks

¼ cup [60 ml] heavy cream

1 Tbsp unsalted butter, at room temperature

1 Tbsp Horlicks or malted milk powder

Pinch kosher salt

DIGESTIVE COOKIES

1½ cups [210 g] whole-wheat flour

¾ cup [90 g] powdered sugar

½ cup [113 g] unsalted butter, cubed, cold

1 tsp kosher salt

1 tsp baking powder

¼ cup [60 ml] whole milk, cold

1 To make the Horlicks ganache, in a small bowl, combine the **milk chocolate** and **cream.** Heat in the microwave in 30 second increments, stirring in between, until melted. Add the **butter** and whisk in by hand until smooth. Add the **Horlicks** and **salt** and whisk to combine until no streaks remain. Place a piece of plastic wrap directly touching the surface and place in the refrigerator for 1 hour to chill.

2 To make the digestive cookies, in the bowl of a stand mixer fitted with the paddle attachment, combine the **flour, powdered sugar, butter, salt,** and **baking powder.** Paddle on medium speed until it resembles a coarse meal with butter chunks the size of lentils. Scrape down the sides of the bowl, and with the mixer running on medium-low speed, drizzle in the **milk.** Continue to mix until the dough just comes together. Depending on the size of your mixer bowl, it may look more like a pebbly streusel dough. As long as the dough sticks when clumped together, it's fine.

3 Divide the dough in half and place one portion in between two pieces of parchment paper roughly measuring 12 by 16 in [30.5 by 40.5 cm]. Roll it out to ⅛ in [3 mm] thick, mimicking the shape of the parchment. Place on a baking sheet and put it in the refrigerator to chill for 30 minutes. Repeat with the other portion of dough.

4 Preheat the oven to 350°F [180°C]. Working with one baking sheet at a time, peel off one side of parchment, gently lay it back on the dough, flip, and peel the other side off. Use a 2 in [5 cm] fluted circle cutter to stamp out cookies. Place the cut cookies onto a parchment-lined baking sheet. Use a small fork to dock holes on each cookie. Repeat with the other sheet of dough. Gather the scraps together and reroll them once more to get more cookies.

5 Bake the cookies until lightly golden brown around the edges, about 12 minutes. Allow to cool on the baking sheets or wire racks.

6 Check on the ganache; you want it to be the consistency of soft butter so you can pipe it. Give it a stir until smooth. If It's too loose, allow it to chill more until you get the desired consistency. Transfer the ganache to a disposable piping bag and cut

cont'd

a ¼ in [6 mm] opening at the tip. Grab a cookie and flip it over, pipe a dime-sized mound of ganache, and top with another cookie, gently pressing so the ganache fills out to the edges. You can eat them straight away, but the ganache will probably ooze out. It is best to allow the cookies to sit out at room temperature, uncovered, for at least 6 hours so the ganache can set and become firm.

Pro Tips & Storage

- The fully assembled cookie sandwiches can be stored in airtight containers for up to 4 days at room temperature or 1 week in the refrigerator.

- The cookie dough can be made in advance and stored, wrapped in plastic wrap or rolled between parchment paper, for up to 2 days in the refrigerator or 3 months in the freezer.

- The ganache can be made in advance and stored in an airtight container for up to 4 days in the refrigerator.

- Try swapping out the filling for Ovaltine Ganache (page 174).

- You can cut them with any size or shape cookie cutter. You can make plain digestive cookies by using a 3 in [7.5 cm] circle cutter and rolling the dough thicker to ¼ in [6 mm]. Obviously, they will take a couple more minutes to bake. Try coating the tops with Pâte à Glacer (page 163) and placing them in the fridge to set.

Fig and Marzipan Mooncakes
Cantonese-Style Baked Mooncakes

Typically, mooncakes are made with a sweet baked dough on the outside and filled with either red bean or lotus seed paste and salted duck yolks to represent the full moon. Growing up, there was no shortage of fancy tins filled with mooncakes around the house during Mid-Autumn Festival. I remember going to family gatherings where there were mooncakes galore, always cut into quarters so everyone could take a little bite. My parents always made a fuss about getting the piece with the most egg yolks in it—it would bring them good luck, they said. Truthfully, I never really enjoyed the taste of traditional mooncakes (gasp!).

While working for a restaurant in New York City, I created my own collection of mooncakes in flavors that people (meaning myself) would actually enjoy, and this was one of them.

YIELD: Makes 8 mooncakes

MOONCAKE DOUGH

2⅔ cups [335 g] all-purpose flour

⅔ cup [230 g] honey

⅓ cup [80 ml] vegetable oil

1 tsp kosher salt

1 tsp lye water (see Pro Tips)

MARZIPAN

1⅔ cups [200 g] powdered sugar

1½ cups [180 g] blanched almond flour

3 Tbsp almond extract

1 large egg white

½ tsp kosher salt

¼ tsp rose water (optional)

8 fresh whole figs, tops trimmed

EGG WASH

1 large egg

2 large egg yolks

1 Tbsp whole milk

¼ tsp kosher salt

1   To make the mooncake dough, in the bowl of a stand mixer fitted with the paddle attachment, combine the **all-purpose flour, honey, vegetable oil, salt,** and **lye water.**

Mix on medium speed until it forms a dough, about 2 minutes; it will be sticky.

2   Wrap the dough in plastic wrap and place in the refrigerator for at least 30 minutes to chill.

3   Meanwhile, make the marzipan. In the bowl of a food processor, combine the **powdered sugar, almond flour, almond extract, egg white, salt,** and **rose water,** if using. Pulse until it comes together into a ball.

4   Scrape out the marzipan onto a piece of plastic wrap. Roll it up tightly into a log and place in the refrigerator to chill for at least 30 minutes.

5   Spray or spread a tiny bit of oil onto a work surface and place a piece of plastic wrap on top. The oil will help the plastic wrap stay in place. The dough is sticky, and it is much easier to work with on plastic. It is also helpful to wear latex gloves or oil your hands to prevent sticking.

Divide the chilled dough into eight equal [70 g] portions and roll each into a ball. Set aside.

6   Divide the marzipan into eight equal [50 g] pieces. Flatten each piece of marzipan into a disc and place a fig in the center. Gather the edges of the marzipan and wrap around the fig. Repeat with the rest.

7   Dust the work surface with some flour. Flatten a ball of dough into a disc about ¼ in [6 mm] thick and place a ball of marzipan in the center. Wrap the dough around the marzipan ball and pinch the edges together to seal. Roll the whole thing into a ball once more to make sure the dough and marzipan are sealed tightly. Repeat with the rest.

8   Add some flour to a bowl. Dunk a 2.6 in [6.7 cm] wide mooncake mold (see Pro Tips) into the flour and tap off any excess. Place a dough ball in the mold and flatten it with the palm of your hand to fill it out. If there is any excess, trim it off with a paring knife. Unmold it onto

cont'd

a parchment-lined baking sheet. Repeat with the rest, leaving at least 2 in [5 cm] of space in between each mooncake on the baking sheet. Place the tray of mooncakes in the freezer for 5 to 10 minutes. Freezing will help the mooncakes retain their shape and design while baking. If you don't have mooncake molds and you are thinking you really want to eat mooncakes that look like a thick hockey puck, then you can just lightly flatten the dough balls using the palm of your hand and proceed.

9　Preheat the oven to 375°F [190°C].

10　To make the egg wash, in a small bowl, whisk together the egg, egg yolks, milk, and salt until smooth.

11　Remove the mooncakes from the freezer and apply two coats of egg wash using a pastry brush. Bake until deep amber brown, 15 to 20 minutes. Let cool completely on the tray or wire rack.

Pro Tips & Storage

- This recipe uses a 2.6 in [6.7 cm] round mooncake mold, which can be purchased at your favorite online marketplace (see the Tools & Equipment section).

- Whole baked mooncakes can be stored in airtight containers for up to 1 week in the refrigerator or 3 months in the freezer.

- Mooncake dough can be made in advance and kept wrapped in plastic wrap for up to 1 week in the refrigerator or 3 months in the freezer.

- Marzipan can be made in advance and kept wrapped in plastic wrap for up to 2 weeks in the refrigerator or 3 months in the freezer.

- This marzipan can be used in any recipe that calls for it, but if you are not baking it, be aware that it contains raw eggs. If this is a concern, you can use pasteurized egg whites.

- Lye water can be found in most Asian markets and online, but if it's unavailable, you can make your own: combine 1 cup [240 ml] of water and ½ tsp of baking soda in a small pot and boil for 8 minutes. Cool before using.

- Try swapping out the fig for other fruits like apples, pears, mangoes, pineapple, peaches, plums, and so on. Use a large melon baller or small cookie scoop to form perfectly round balls of fruit.

- For more traditional mooncakes, swap out the marzipan for red bean paste or lotus paste and the figs for salted egg yolks.

Audris's Black Sesame Ricciarelli

Chewy Black Sesame Almond Cookies

While living in Florence, Italy, I was able to visit the medieval city of Siena, where I indulged in a box of the city's signature treats, called ricciarelli. These almond cookies have a powdered sugar crackly top with a soft and chewy interior. One year I brought a box home for Christmas along with a recipe I got from Le Cordon Bleu while taking courses there. My family devoured the cookies, and my sister, Audris, and I made them pretty much nonstop for the next year.

Fast forward a million years to another Christmas. My sister brought over these black sesame ricciarelli that she had invented, and I ate them in awe. They were delectable. They have the same chew, with a thin caramelized outer shell, but are amplified by the nuttiness from the black sesame. Luckily, my sister gave me permission to share her recipe for these cookies you will not be able to stop eating.

YIELD: Makes 18 cookies

2 large egg whites

¾ cup [90 g] powdered sugar

½ cup + 2 Tbsp [130 g] granulated sugar

2½ Tbsp black sesame paste

1 tsp almond extract

1 cup [120 g] almond flour

Pinch kosher salt

Black sesame seeds, to garnish (optional)

1 In a medium mixing bowl, whisk together the **egg whites, powdered sugar,** and **granulated sugar** until thick and opaque, 2 to 3 minutes. It should have the viscosity of a thick syrup. Add the **black sesame paste** and **almond extract** and whisk until smooth. Use a rubber spatula to stir in the **almond flour** and **salt** until the dough is smooth and no streaks remain.

2 Transfer the dough into a bowl, and, using spoons or a 1 oz cookie scoop, portion the dough into 2 Tbsp balls.

3 Preheat the oven to 325°F [165°C]. Place the balls on a parchment-lined baking sheet and sprinkle **black sesame seeds** on top, if desired. Bake until very lightly browned on the bottom and set on the top, 16 to 18 minutes. Allow to cool on the baking sheet or a wire rack.

Pro Tips & Storage

- The cookie dough can be kept wrapped in plastic wrap then stored in a zip-top bag for up to 3 months in the freezer.

- The baked cookies can be stored in zip-top bags or an airtight container for up to 3 days at room temperature, 1 week in the refrigerator, or 3 months in the freezer.

- Try swapping out the black sesame paste for tahini or another nut butter.

Mochi Lamington

I grew up in a suburb of Los Angeles where I was one of maybe ten Asian kids. My last name was always misspelled as Lamb because nobody had ever heard of a Lam before. In high school, it got even worse because everyone thought my parents had named me after Clarice in *The Silence of the Lambs*. If I saw either of my names typed out anywhere, I would get really excited, as if I finally had been represented. I took a trip with my sister to Australia once for my friend's wedding, and at one of the first bakeries we visited, we noticed a chocolate cube coated in desiccated coconut called a LAMington. As it turns out, it's one of Australia's national treats. For my version, I use Chinese chiffon cake as the base, filled with an ethereal raspberry cream, then wrap the whole thing like a gift in chewy chocolate mochi rolled in sweetened coconut flakes.

YIELD: Makes 6 lamingtons

CHIFFON CAKE

3 large egg whites

¼ tsp kosher salt

½ cup [100 g] granulated sugar

3 large egg yolks

3 Tbsp whole milk

2½ Tbsp vegetable oil

1 tsp vanilla extract

¾ cup + 1 Tbsp [100 g] cake flour, sifted

¼ tsp baking powder

RASPBERRY CREAM

1½ cups [360 ml] heavy cream

¼ cup [85 g] raspberry preserves

1 cup [120 g] fresh raspberries, for garnish (optional)

CHOCOLATE MOCHI

2¼ cups + 3 Tbsp [270 g] Mochiko or glutinous rice flour

1⅓ cups [320 ml] whole milk

¼ cup + 3 Tbsp [95 g] granulated sugar

2 Tbsp + 2 tsp vegetable oil

1½ Tbsp Dutch-process cocoa powder

¼ tsp kosher salt

2 cups [200 g] coconut flakes

1 Preheat the oven to 350°F [180°C].

2 To make the chiffon cake, in the bowl of a stand mixer fitted with the whisk attachment, combine the **egg whites** and **salt**. Whisk on medium speed until frothy, then add ¼ cup [50 g] of the **sugar**. Continue to whip on medium-high speed until stiff peaks form, 2 to 3 minutes. Set aside.

3 In a large mixing bowl, combine the **egg yolks** with the remaining ¼ cup [50 g] of sugar. Whisk until pale and fluffy, about 2 minutes. Add the **milk**, **oil**, and **vanilla** and whisk to combine. Add the **flour** and **baking powder** and mix until no streaks remain.

4 Add about one third of the egg whites to the egg yolk mixture and fold using a whisk to lighten the batter. Add another third and gently fold it in with as few strokes as possible to combine. Add the final third and fold until no streaks remain. Try not to deflate the batter.

5 Pour the batter into a parchment-lined 9 by 13 in [23 by 33 cm] baking pan and smooth out to an even layer, making sure to get into the corners and all way to the edges of the pan. Bake until the cake is cooked through and bounces back to the touch, about 20 minutes. Allow to cool completely in the pan.

6 To make the raspberry cream, in the bowl of a stand mixer fitted with the whisk attachment, combine the **cream** and **raspberry preserves** and whip until stiff peaks form. Do not overwhip. Set aside 2 Tbsp of the whipped cream and 6 of the **fresh raspberries** in the refrigerator to garnish, if desired. Add the rest of the fresh raspberries to the whipped cream and gently fold to incorporate.

7 Cut the sheet of cake crosswise in half so you have two pieces measuring roughly 6 by 9 in [15 by 23 cm]. Spread an even ½ in [13 mm] layer of raspberry cream on one side. Place the other half of the cake on top like a sandwich. Place the whole

cont'd

thing in the freezer for 4 hours. This will make the cutting and shaping easier.

8 To make the chocolate mochi, in a medium bowl, whisk together the Mochiko, milk, sugar, oil, cocoa powder, and salt. Cover with plastic wrap, leaving a small vent on one side. Microwave for 2 minutes. Remove the plastic wrap and stir. Re-cover loosely with the plastic wrap and microwave again for 1 minute. Using a rubber spatula scrape the dough from underneath and fold it on top of itself. Go around the bowl a couple times, continuing to fold and stir. It is cooked when it looks like a rubber ball of dough. It will be tacky and sticky but not goopy. If your mochi is still not cooked through, place it back in the microwave in 30 second increments until it is done.

9 Transfer the mochi to the bowl of a stand mixer fitted with the dough hook attachment. Knead on medium speed until smooth, about 7 minutes. It will look like a very silky and sticky batter; it will firm up as it cools.

10 Scrape out the mochi onto a work surface lightly greased with nonstick spray or vegetable oil. It should be a nonporous surface like marble or stainless steel. If this is not available to you, you can cover your surface with plastic wrap and grease on top of the plastic. Grease your hands and pat the top of the mochi to coat. Allow it to cool for 10 minutes.

11 Lightly grease your hands again and pat the mochi out to a rectangle. Grease a rolling pin or use a fondant rolling pin and roll the mochi out to a 12 by 16 in [30.5 by 40.5 cm] rectangle ⅛ in [3 mm] thick. Cut it into six 5 in [13 cm] squares.

12 Trim ½ to 1 in [13 mm to 2.5 cm] off the edges of the cake so you end up with a 4 by 6 in [10 by 15 cm] block. Cut it in half lengthwise and in thirds crosswise so you have six cake cubes measuring 2 in [5 cm] square.

13 Take one cake cube, rotate it, and place it in the center of a mochi square so it looks like a diamond within a square. Fold the flaps of mochi over the cake like you are wrapping a present. Pinch all the seams to seal and trim off any excess so it still looks like a cube. Repeat with the rest.

14 Add the coconut flakes to a small bowl. Dunk a mochi into the coconut flakes to generously coat, pressing lightly so the coconut sticks. With the reserved raspberry cream, pipe a tiny rosette on top and garnish with a reserved raspberry, if desired. Repeat with the rest. Serve slightly chilled.

Pro Tips & Storage

- The assembled lamingtons can be kept in an airtight container for up to 4 days in the refrigerator.

- The cake can be made in advance and stored flat in the baking pan, double wrapped in plastic wrap, for up to 3 months in the freezer. It can also be assembled with the raspberry cream and kept flat, double wrapped as a block, for up to 3 months in the freezer.

- If you want to make regular lamingtons, you can skip making the mochi and dip each cake cube in Pâte à Glacer (page 163) before rolling in coconut flakes.

- The mochi can be stored flat in the baking pan and double wrapped for up to 3 days in the refrigerator.

- Try wrapping the mochi around small scoops of Condensed Milk Ice Cream (page 166) or the Vietnamese coffee variation (page 163). These can be stored in airtight containers for up to 3 months in the freezer.

- To make plain mochi, omit the cocoa powder.

Bolo Bao Cream Puffs

Bolo-Topped Cream Puffs, Royal Milk Tea Diplomat & Boba

Many years ago, I was asked to make a treat that represented Hong Kong for a food festival, and I immediately thought of bolo bao, or pineapple buns. There are certain foods and dishes that exist in one form or another no matter where you are in the world. I love finding connections between them and understanding the roots, how they traveled, and what they became. Bolo bao is one of those foods; a version of a soft, sweet bread with a sweet cookie top exists in multiple countries. Although France has no shortage of sweet breads, they also have cream puffs that are frequently topped with craquelin, what they call their crunchy cookie top. Using that as my inspiration here, I filled it with a royal milk tea diplomat, which is pastry cream plus whipped cream, and boba.

YIELD: Makes 12 large cream puffs

ROYAL MILK TEA DIPLOMAT

2 cups [480 ml] whole milk

6 black tea bags or 2 Tbsp loose tea leaves

½ cup [100 g] granulated sugar

1 large egg

2 large egg yolks

¼ cup [35 g] cornstarch

2 tsp vanilla extract

½ tsp kosher salt

1 cup [240 ml] heavy cream, cold

½ cup [70 g] boba, uncooked (optional)

1 recipe Bolo Topping (page 40)

1 recipe Egg Wash (page 35)

CHOUX

6 Tbsp [85 g] unsalted butter

½ tsp kosher salt

½ tsp granulated sugar

1 cup [150 g] all-purpose flour

4 large eggs

1 To make the diplomat, in a small pot over medium-high heat, bring the milk to a scald—small bubbles around the edges, right before boiling. Add the tea, remove from the heat, and let steep, covered, for 20 minutes. Pour the milk tea through a fine-mesh sieve into a medium pot, squeezing out the tea bags or using the back of a spoon to press all the liquid out. Whisk in the sugar and bring it back to a scald over medium-high heat.

2 While it's heating, in a medium mixing bowl, combine the egg, egg yolks, cornstarch, vanilla, and salt. Whisk by hand until pale and fluffy, about 1 minute.

3 Slowly pour the hot milk tea into the eggs, whisking constantly to prevent the eggs from scrambling.

4 Return the egg mixture to the pot and continue to whisk over medium-high heat until it starts to boil and thicken, 3 to 5 minutes. Transfer the custard to a bowl and place a piece of plastic wrap directly touching surface to prevent a skin from forming. Place the bowl over an ice bath to cool for 30 minutes, then refrigerate for at least 30 minutes more until fully chilled.

5 In the bowl of a stand mixer fitted with the whisk attachment, whip the heavy cream to stiff peaks. Transfer to a large bowl and set aside. Place the chilled milk tea custard into the mixer bowl and switch to a paddle attachment. Mix until smooth. Scrape down the sides of the bowl and add the whipped cream. Switch it back to the whisk attachment and mix on medium-low speed until fully combined and no streaks remain. Transfer it back into the large bowl, cover with plastic wrap, and refrigerate until ready to use.

cont'd

6   Make the **boba** according to the package instructions, if using. Transfer to a bowl and refrigerate until ready to use.

7   Make the **bolo topping**, steps 8 to 11.

8   Make the **egg wash**.

9   To make the choux, in a medium pot bring ¾ cup [180 ml] of water, the **butter, salt,** and **sugar** to a boil over medium-high heat. Make sure the water and butter are at a rolling boil before adding the flour, otherwise it won't work. Add the **flour,** and stir until it comes together into a ball, about 1 minute. Lower the heat to medium and continue to stir and smash the dough to cook some of the moisture out, 3 to 4 minutes. There should be a thin film of dough on the bottom of the pan.

10 Turn the dough out into the bowl of a stand mixer fitted with the paddle attachment. Paddle the dough on medium-high speed to release the steam, 1 to 2 minutes.

11 Add the **eggs** one at a time, allowing the dough to come back together before adding the next. Scrape down the sides of the bowl and mix until everything is completely combined and smooth. The dough should be glossy, and you should be able to draw a line through it with your finger and have it slowly fill in on itself. Transfer to a piping bag fitted with a ½ in [13 mm] circle tip (I use Ateco 805).

12 Line two 13 by 17 in [33 by 43 cm] baking sheets with parchment paper. Pipe six 2½ in [6 cm] diameter mounds of batter on each sheet, leaving at least 2 in [5 cm] of space between each one. Hold the pastry bag vertically ¾ in [2 cm] away from the paper and gently squeeze without moving the piping bag. When you reach the desired size, quickly twist and flick the piping bag so you have more of a flat top than a peak.

13 Brush the tops of the choux with one coat of egg wash and set aside.

14 Preheat the oven to 400°F [200°C].

15 Remove the sheet of bolo dough from the refrigerator, peel off one side of parchment paper, gently lay it back onto the dough, flip it onto your work surface, and peel off the other side of parchment. Use a 3 in [7.5 cm] circle cookie cutter to cut out twelve discs. Save the scraps and reroll them again between two sheets of parchment paper to cut more discs, if needed.

16 Place one disc on top of a mound of choux, then brush the top with another coat of egg wash and repeat with the rest. Bake for 15 minutes, then lower the heat to 375°F [190°C]. Continue to bake until the tops are dark golden brown and crackly and the puffs are well browned and cooked through, about 25 minutes more. Remove from the oven and let cool completely on the baking sheets or a wire rack.

17 Use a paring knife or chopstick to gently poke holes in the bottom of each puff.

18 Drain the cooked boba and lightly dab dry with a paper towel. Using a rubber spatula, carefully fold the boba into the chilled milk tea diplomat until evenly dispersed. Transfer to a piping bag fitted with a ½ in [13 mm] piping tip. The tip should be at least as big as the boba.

19 Pipe diplomat into each puff until it feels heavy and starts to overflow. Scrape off any excess filling and serve.

Pro Tips & Storage

- The filled cream puffs are best eaten the day of. The unfilled shells can be stored in zip-top bags or airtight containers for up to 3 months in the freezer.

- Don't skimp on cooking the dough out over the stovetop. This is an important step, as we want to cook out some of the moisture so we can replace it with the eggs. Stir and smash the dough against the bottom of the pan to dry it out evenly. You want to make sure there is a thin film of crusted dough on the bottom of the pan before taking it off the heat.

- To make plain cream puffs, leave off the bolo topping. Try swapping out the filling for Pastry Cream (page 117).

- Turn the cream puffs into profiteroles by cutting them in half, placing a scoop of Condensed Milk Ice Cream (page 166) or the Vietnamese coffee variation (page 163) in the center, then topping them with Hot Fudge (page 163).

Yin Yeung Crullers
Hong Kong Milk Tea & Coffee–Glazed Crullers

There are these specific donuts that I have only ever been able to find in Hong Kong. They were light and fluffy, very pale, and had a spongier texture than most donuts. They came coated in sugar and were filled with a surprise—usually a piece of banana or red bean paste. I had to use the Google machine to figure out what they are even called. Hong Kong sugar puffs is what I found out, but it still doesn't quite match my memory. So, I made my own version, in cruller form, glazed with flavors from a traditional morning beverage called yin yeung, which is Hong Kong milk tea with a shot of coffee. The process is pretty much identical to pâte à choux, the dough responsible for éclairs and cream puffs, only it uses egg whites in addition to whole eggs.

YIELD: Makes 6 donuts

HONG KONG MILK TEA GLAZE

½ cup [120 ml] whole milk

4 black tea bags or 1½ Tbsp loose tea leaves

1 cup [120 g] powdered sugar

2 Tbsp unsalted butter, melted

CRULLERS

6 cups [1.4 L] vegetable oil

4 Tbsp [55 g] unsalted butter

2 Tbsp granulated sugar

½ tsp kosher salt

1¼ cups [190 g] all-purpose flour

1 large egg

3 large egg whites

COFFEE GLAZE

1 cup [120 g] powdered sugar

3 Tbsp whole milk

2 Tbsp unsalted butter, melted

2 tsp instant coffee or espresso powder

1 To make the milk tea glaze, bring the **milk** just to a boil, then turn the heat down and add the **tea**. Let it simmer until reduced by half, 5 to 8 minutes. Remove from the heat and steep, covered, at room temperature for another 20 minutes to 1 hour.

2 Meanwhile, make the crullers. Prepare a piping bag fitted with a ⅝ in [1.5 cm] star tip (Ateco 828). Cut six 4 in [10 cm] squares of parchment paper. Set aside.

3 In a large heavy-bottomed pot over high heat, bring the **vegetable oil** to 350°F [180°C].

4 While the oil is heating, in a medium heavy-bottomed pot, bring 1 cup [240 ml] of water, the **butter, sugar,** and **salt** to a rolling boil. Turn the heat down to medium and add the **flour**. Stir using a wooden spoon until it comes together in a ball.

5 Continue to smash and stir the dough around the bottom and sides of the pot to dry it out, 2 to 3 minutes more.

6 Transfer the dough to the bowl of a stand mixer fitted with the paddle attachment. Mix the dough on medium speed to release the steam, 1 to 2 minutes.

7 Add the **egg** and **egg whites** one at a time, allowing the dough to come back together between additions. Scrape down the sides and bottom of the bowl and mix until smooth and glossy, about 30 seconds more. Transfer the dough into the prepared piping bag.

8 Gather the parchment squares and pipe a circle within each square, about ½ in [13 mm] away from the edges.

cont'd

9　Carefully lift a cruller by two opposing corners of the parchment paper. Once you are over the pot, release one hand, holding the paper by only one corner now, and gently lower the whole thing, donut-side down, into the heated oil. Work in batches, frying two or three crullers at a time without overcrowding the pot.

10　After about 2 minutes, the donuts will float to the top. Use tongs to carefully peel off the parchment squares and discard. Fry until dark golden brown, 3 to 4 minutes on each side, 6 to 8 minutes total. Using tongs or a spider, remove the donuts from the oil and allow to cool completely on a wire rack or a paper towel–lined plate. Meanwhile, finish the glazes.

11　To finish the milk tea glaze, strain the tea-steeped milk through a fine-mesh sieve into a small mixing bowl. Whisk in the **powdered sugar** and **butter**.

12　To make the coffee glaze, in a small mixing bowl, whisk together the **powdered sugar, milk, butter,** and **instant coffee.**

13　Take a cruller and dunk one side halfway into the milk tea glaze and the other side in the coffee glaze. Place it back onto the wire rack to set. Repeat with the rest.

Pro Tips & Storage

- The donuts should be eaten the day of.
- They can be prepiped onto parchment squares and frozen in a single layer on a baking sheet, wrapped in plastic, for up to 3 months. Once they have completely frozen in a single layer, you can transfer them to a zip-top bag to save space.
- Keep an eye on the oil temperature while frying, especially if you are frying straight from the freezer. It is normal for the temp to dip once you put them in, but if it doesn't rise back up, you will need to regulate it. You want to keep it as close to 350°F [180°C] as possible.
- If you want a smoother look, glaze the donuts while they are still a little warm. If you want the glaze to set thicker, wait until the donuts have completely cooled before glazing.
- You can also adjust the thickness of the glazes by adding more milk 1 tsp at a time to thin it out or powdered sugar 1 Tbsp at a time to thicken.

Black & White Mochi Munchkins

At the time of writing this book, I have been in NYC for fourteen years—my longest stretch ever of living in a single city. When I first moved here, I stayed with my friend Stephanie, whose favorite sweet treat was a black and white cookie, one of the Big Apple's iconic foods. Another thing that's synonymous with NYC, in my opinion, is Dunkin'. One of their most iconic treats are their donut holes, which they call Munchkins.

I have a love-hate relationship with the city, but overall, I have to be grateful for the place that launched my career as a chef. For that, I wanted to create a treat that will always remind me of the city that never sleeps.

YIELD: Makes 24 donut holes

MUNCHKINS

⅔ cup [160 ml] whole milk

¼ cup [50 g] granulated sugar

2 Tbsp unsalted butter

¼ tsp kosher salt

2 cups [220 g] Mochiko or glutinous rice flour

2 Tbsp tapioca starch

1 large egg, lightly beaten

2 tsp baking powder

6 cups [1.4 L] vegetable oil

VANILLA GLAZE

2 cups [240 g] powdered sugar

¼ cup [60 ml] whole milk

4 Tbsp [55 g] unsalted butter, melted

1 tsp vanilla extract

CHOCOLATE GLAZE

2 cups [240 g] powdered sugar

¼ cup + 1 Tbsp [75 ml] whole milk

4 Tbsp [55 g] unsalted butter, melted

2 Tbsp black cocoa powder or Dutch-process cocoa powder

1. To make the munchkins, in a medium pot over medium-high heat, heat the milk, sugar, butter, 2 Tbsp of water, and the salt and bring to a boil.

2. Add the Mochiko and tapioca starch. Turn the heat to low and stir until it becomes a firm and goopy ball, about 2 minutes. Initially it will look very clumpy and dry; just continue to stir, fold, and smear the dough against the sides and bottom of the pot until it comes together.

3. Transfer the dough into the bowl of a stand mixer fitted with the paddle attachment. Knead on medium speed to release the steam, about 2 minutes.

4. Scrape down the sides of the bowl and add about half the egg. Continue to mix on medium speed until the dough comes back together, 1 minute. Scrape down the bowl again, add the rest of the egg, and continue to knead until smooth and combined, about 1 minute more. Scrape down the bowl and add the

baking powder and mix to combine, 1 minute. The dough will be very sticky. Transfer to a bowl and cover with plastic wrap.

5. In a large heavy-bottomed pot over high heat, bring the vegetable oil to 350°F [180°C].

6. While the oil heats, scoop out 1½ Tbsp of dough and roll it into a ball. Set aside and repeat with the rest. Keep the balls covered in plastic wrap to prevent them from drying out.

7. Carefully lower the donut balls into the hot oil. Working in batches, fry five or six donuts at a time without overcrowding the pot.

8. Fry for 2 to 3 minutes on each side until golden brown, 5 to 6 minutes total. Using tongs or a spider, carefully remove the donuts onto a paper towel–lined plate to cool completely. Meanwhile, make the glazes.

cont'd

9   To make the vanilla glaze, in a small mixing bowl, whisk together the powdered sugar, milk, butter, and vanilla.

10 To make the chocolate glaze, in a small mixing bowl, whisk together the powdered sugar, milk, butter, and cocoa powder.

11 Gently stab a fork into the side of a donut. Dip one side of the donut in the vanilla glaze, trying to create a straight edge in the center of the donut, and tapping off any excess glaze. Flip it to the other side and dip it into the chocolate glaze, trying to meet the straight edge of the vanilla glaze, tapping off any excess. Set it down on a plate or wire rack to set and repeat with the rest.

Pro Tips & Storage

- The donuts should be eaten the day of.
- It's important to keep stirring the dough over the stovetop until it becomes a ball to activate the "chewy."
- Keep an eye on the oil temperature while frying. It is normal for the temp to dip once you put them in, but if it doesn't rise back up, you will need to regulate it. You want to keep it as close to 350°F [180°C] as possible.
- Try using a ¾ in [2 cm] circle cutter to cut holes in the centers for a more traditional donut shape. You can also fry the holes!
- Roll the dough into tablespoon-sized balls for perfectly round donuts.
- Try glazing with Hong Kong Milk Tea Glaze (page 209), Coffee Glaze (page 209), Ovaltine Ganache (page 174), Horlicks Ganache (page 192), or Condensed Milk Glaze (page 90).

Ferrero Mochi Bomboloncini
Ferrero Rocher–Filled Fried Sesame Balls

This recipe holds a lot of importance for me, as I can recall my mother frying up batches of jian dui for Chinese New Year, and this version of them has become one of my signature desserts. Technically speaking, it is a mochi—and a bomboloncino too, if we are relying on the definition that translates to golf ball–sized donut. But truly, this is my mother's recipe for jian dui.

I created a similar version for an Italian-Japanese restaurant in NYC, where I called them Nutella mochi bomboloncini. The prep for that version is a little more involved, so for this recipe, I thought, why not just stuff it with an entire ball of Ferrero Rocher? What some people may not know is that these nutty truffles wrapped in gold foil are prized in many Asian households.

YIELD: Makes 8 bomboloncini

¾ cup [150 g] granulated sugar

1¼ cup [140 g] Mochiko or glutinous rice flour

8 Ferrero Rocher chocolates, unwrapped

4 cups [960 ml] vegetable oil

½ cup [70 g] white sesame seeds

1 In a small pot bring ⅓ cup + 1 Tbsp [95 ml] of water and ¼ cup [50 g] of the sugar to a boil.

2 In a medium mixing bowl, add the Mochiko. Pour the sugary syrup into the rice flour and stir using chopsticks or a rubber spatula until it forms a shaggy mass. Knead by hand until smooth, 2 to 3 minutes. Cover the dough loosely with a piece of plastic wrap and allow it to rest for 15 minutes.

3 Roll the dough into a log and cut into eight equal [30 g] pieces. Take one piece, roll it into a ball, and then flatten into a 3 in [7.5 cm] disc. Place a Ferrero Rocher in the center and wrap the dough around, pinching the seams to seal. Roll into a smooth ball once again and set aside. Repeat with the rest.

4 In a large heavy-bottomed pot over high heat, bring the vegetable oil to 330°F [165°C].

5 Set up for dipping: Fill a small bowl with water and place the sesame seeds in a separate bowl. Dunk one ball into the water and shake off any excess, then roll in the sesame seeds to coat. Repeat with the rest.

6 Fry in two batches, four at a time, until golden brown and crispy on the outside, 10 to 12 minutes. Roll the balls around every now and then to make sure all the sides get fried. Keep an eye on the oil temperature, regulating when necessary.

7 Place the remaining ½ cup [100 g] of sugar in a small bowl. Using a spider or tongs, transfer the bomboloncini to a paper towel–lined plate. While still warm, toss each one into the sugar to coat. Serve immediately.

Pro Tips & Storage

- These are best eaten the day of.
- The balls can be assembled in advance and stored flat on a baking sheet double wrapped in plastic wrap for up to 3 days in the refrigerator or 3 months in the freezer. Frying times will obviously be longer.
- Try swapping out the Ferrero Rocher for balls of red bean paste, lotus seed paste, Black Sesame Filling (page 82), Hazelnut Praliné (page 160), Ovaltine Ganache (page 174), Horlicks Ganache (page 192), or Marzipan (page 195).

Gochujang-Furikake Caramel Popcorn

Popcorn is the perfect snack. At The Baking Bean, I sold two flavors of caramel popcorn wholesale to various markets and bakeries around the United States. I sold a Mexican-inspired version of caramel corn, which had ancho, chipotle, and spicy mango bits—that was my favorite. Here I swap out the Mexican spices for gochujang, a Korean fermented chili paste that adds a sweet spice and funk to the popcorn. The dusting of furikake, a Japanese dry condiment that is typically used for seasoning rice, enhances the flavors of the gochujang.

There are many types of furikake. Here I use the nori komi kind, which is a blend of seaweed, sesame seeds, sugar, and salt. If you are a furikake connoisseur, feel free to experiment with other mixes. The result is complex, addictive, and unexpectedly delicious.

YIELD: Makes 3 quarts

⅓ cup [80 g] popcorn kernels

1 cup [200 g] granulated sugar

1 Tbsp light corn syrup

5 Tbsp [70 g] unsalted butter, cubed

1 Tbsp gochujang

½ tsp baking soda

½ tsp kosher salt

3 Tbsp nori komi furikake

1 Line a baking sheet with parchment paper. Pop the kernels using the method of your choice; I use an air popper. Grab the largest mixing bowl you have and grease with non-stick spray or use a paper towel to wipe vegetable oil all over the inside of the bowl. Dig your hands into the popped corn like a claw machine and shake out any unpopped kernels, transferring the popcorn into the greased bowl. Unpopped kernels will break your teeth if not removed.

2 In medium saucepan, combine the sugar, ⅓ cup [80 ml] of water, and the corn syrup. Wet your fingers and wipe any sugar crystals from the sides of the pot. Turn the heat to medium-high and cook until the temperature reaches 375°F [190°C], 10 to 12 minutes.

3 Lower the heat to medium and carefully add the butter, gochujang, baking soda, and salt; whisk until homogenous. Be careful, as the caramel will puff up and splatter. Quickly pour the caramel over the popcorn. Use two rubber spatulas to toss like a salad until everything is evenly coated.

4 Pour the caramel corn onto the prepared baking sheet and break it up using a rubber spatula. As soon as it's cool enough to handle, finish breaking it up with your hands. Sprinkle the furikake over the top and toss once more to incorporate. Allow to cool completely before serving.

Pro Tips & Storage

- The caramel popcorn can be stored in an airtight container or zip-top bag for up to 3 weeks in a cool and dry environment.
- Try adding peanuts or coconut flakes to the mix.

Miso Caramel–Covered Marshmallows

Homemade marshmallows are far superior to the mass manufactured kind. Once you make them, you may never want to go back. They are fresh, tender, and bouncy, plus you can customize them by cutting them into any size you like.

Some of the best marshmallow variations are the old-school caramel-covered ones. Invented by a confectioner from Kentucky in the late 1800s, he called them Modjeskas, in honor of a Shakespearean actress by the same name. For my version, I add red miso to the caramel to add umami and roll it in a traditional Chinese mix of peanuts, coconut, and black sesame.

YIELD: Makes 18 pieces

VANILLA MARSHMALLOWS

1 Tbsp + 1 tsp powdered gelatin

1 cup [200 g] granulated sugar

¼ cup [80 g] light corn syrup

1 large egg white

¼ tsp kosher salt

1 tsp vanilla extract

MISO CARAMEL

⅔ cup [160 ml] heavy cream

⅔ cup [130 g] granulated sugar

3 Tbsp light corn syrup

5 Tbsp [70 g] unsalted butter, at room temperature

1½ Tbsp red miso

1 Tbsp lemon juice

COATING

⅔ cup [65 g] desiccated coconut

⅓ cup [45 g] roasted peanuts, finely ground

⅓ cup [45 g] black sesame seeds, roasted

1   To make the marshmallows, line a 6 in [15 cm] square pan with parchment paper and grease with nonstick spray.

2   In a small dish, place ¼ cup [60 ml] of water and sprinkle over the **gelatin**. Quickly stir until it forms a goopy mass and no dry spots are showing. Set aside to bloom.

3   In a small pot, stir together the **sugar**, ⅓ cup [80 ml] of water, and the **corn syrup**. Bring to a boil over medium-high heat and continue to cook until it reaches 250°F [120°C].

4   While the syrup is cooking, in the bowl of a stand mixer fitted with the whisk attachment, whip the **egg white** and **salt** to medium-stiff peaks. If it's too small of an amount for your mixer, you may have to whisk by hand. Transfer to a small bowl and set aside.

5   Place the bloomed gelatin lump into the mixer bowl fitted with the whisk attachment. Pour the sugar syrup over the gelatin and turn the mixer on medium-low to start. Once it stops sloshing around, turn the speed up to medium-high and continue to whip for 5 minutes. Add the whipped egg white and the

vanilla. Whip until fluffy and stiff, 3 to 5 minutes more. It should hold a peak and not dissolve back into itself. Transfer the marshmallow to the prepared pan and spread it out quickly into an even layer. Spray another piece of parchment paper with nonstick spray and place it directly touching the marshmallow, greased side down. Wrap in plastic wrap and allow it to set on the counter for 8 hours or overnight.

6   To make the miso caramel, line a 9 by 13 in [23 by 33 cm] baking sheet with parchment paper. In a small pot, bring the **cream** to a scald— small bubbles around the edges, right before boiling—over medium-high heat. Set aside.

7   In a very clean medium pot, stir together the **sugar**, ¼ cup [60 ml] of water, and the **corn syrup**. Wet your fingers and wipe down any sugar crystals on the inside of the pot. Without stirring, heat on medium-high to 375°F [190°C], about 7 minutes.

cont'd

8 Lower the heat to medium and carefully add the heated cream and the **butter**. It will bubble up and spatter, so be careful. Whisk together until combined. Continue to cook until it reaches 260°F [125°C]. Add the **miso** and **lemon juice** and whisk until homogeneous. Remove the caramel from the heat and pour it into the prepared baking sheet. Allow to cool for 1 hour at room temperature before transferring to the refrigerator to chill for 2 hours.

9 To make the coating, in a bowl, stir together the **coconut, peanuts,** and **sesame seeds**. Transfer to a plate and spread it out.

10 Remove the marshmallow from the pan and place it on a cutting board. Cut it through the parchment into five 1 in [2.5 cm] strips. Cut two of the marshmallow strips in half.

11 Remove the caramel from the baking sheet and cut it through the parchment into three 5 by 9 in [13 by 23 cm] strips. Place one strip of marshmallow along the long edge of the caramel and place a half strip of marshmallow right up against the other marshmallow to complete the length, peeling off the parchment. Roll the caramel strip up tight and pinch the seam to seal. Repeat with the rest. Eat any leftover marshmallow scraps.

12 Peel the parchment off the caramel log and roll it in the topping to coat. Repeat with the other logs. Cut each log into 1 in [2.5 cm] slices and serve or individually wrap with wax paper.

Pro Tips & Storage

- The finished pieces can be stored, individually wrapped in wax paper, in an airtight container for up to 3 weeks in a cool, dry place.

- The marshmallows can be stored, double wrapped in plastic wrap, for up to 2 weeks at room temperature, 3 weeks in the refrigerator, or 3 months in the freezer.

- The caramel can be made into a sauce by removing from the heat after whisking in the lemon juice in step 8. Store in an airtight container for up to 2 weeks at room temperature or 1 month in the refrigerator. Try making a banana split with the miso caramel sauce, Condensed Milk Ice Cream (page 166), and Hot Fudge (page 163).

- This is my all-purpose marshmallow recipe. Try cutting it into large squares for smores or add them to your hot chocolate.

- The peanuts can be ground in a food processor or finely chopped.

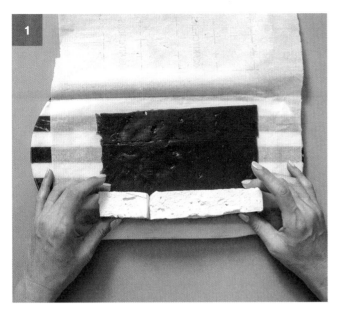

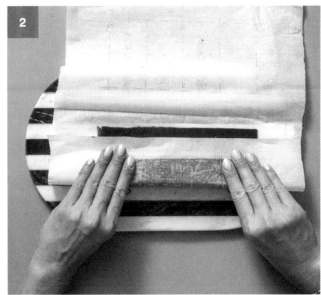

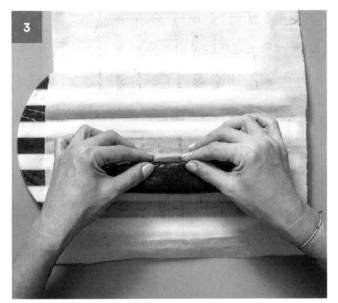

Pistachio, Pineapple & Dragon Fruit Nougat

My love affair with nougat began with a pale blue box from Harrods department store in London. After a long, hard day of shopping, we returned to the hotel room where my sister and I tore the box open. The firm, marshmallowy texture of the nougat was perfect against the nuts and bright red candied cherries. Sadly, the next time we went to London, they were no longer available.

Since then, I have been keeping my eyes peeled for that exact nougat. I tested many nougats while living in France and Italy, but never found one with that same fluffy chew. This recipe is an ode to the original Harrod's nougat that I fell in love with, incorporating Southeast Asian fruits by substituting neon fuchsia dragon fruit for the bright red cherries and pineapple for the citrus peels.

YIELD: Makes 40 pieces

2½ cups [500 g] granulated sugar

1 cup [340 g] good-quality honey

4 large egg whites

¼ tsp kosher salt

2 sheets wafer paper (optional)

¾ cup + 1 Tbsp [100 g] powdered sugar

2 cups [280 g] shelled roasted pistachios

1 cup [170 g] dried pineapple chunks, roughly chopped

1 cup [50 g] freeze-dried dragon fruit or freeze-dried raspberries

1 In a large saucepan, stir together the **sugar, honey,** and ¾ cup [180 ml] of water. Use wet fingertips to wipe down any sugar crystals from the walls of the pot. Cook over medium-high heat until it reaches 320°F [160°C]. It is very important to use a bigger pot than you think; the honey will bubble up very high and overflow if the walls of the pot aren't high enough. It is also important to make sure the pot is very clean or the sugar may crystallize, yielding a different result.

2 Meanwhile, in the bowl of a stand mixer fitted with the whisk attachment, whip the **egg whites** and **salt** to medium peaks.

3 Grease an 8 in [20 cm] square pan with nonstick spray, then line it with parchment paper. If using **wafer paper,** place a sheet on the bottom of the pan. If not using, lightly spray nonstick spray over the top of the parchment as well.

4 When the sugar syrup reaches 320°F [160°C], remove from the heat and set aside. Turn the mixer back on and finish whipping the egg whites to stiff peaks. Lower the speed to medium and slowly drizzle in the sugar syrup in four additions, allowing it to get mixed in before adding the next. Turn the mixer back up to medium-high and continue whipping until stiff and sticky, 10 minutes. Add the **powdered sugar** and mix until fully dissolved and no lumps remain.

5 Scrape down the sides of the bowl and the whisk attachment. Swap out the whisk for the paddle attachment and add the **pistachios, dried pineapple,** and **freeze-dried fruit.** Mix to combine until everything is evenly dispersed.

6 Using a greased bowl scraper or spatula, scrape the nougat out into the prepared pan. Try to spread it to the edges. It will be very thick and fairly stiff. Top with the other wafer paper, if using, and gently press to fill out the pan. If not using, lightly spray another sheet of parchment paper, place it on top of the nougat, and press.

7 Allow to cool for 8 hours or overnight in the refrigerator.

8 Transfer the block of nougat to a cutting board and cut into 1 by 1½ in [2.5 by 4 cm] pieces. Serve as is or wrap them individually using wax paper.

cont'd

Pro Tips & Storage

- Nougat is very sensitive to humidity, so unless you live in a very cool and dry place, I recommend storing the nougat in an airtight container for up to 2 weeks in the refrigerator.

- You can mix in whatever kind of nuts and dried, candied, or freeze-dried fruit you like.

- Please use pure, high-quality, organic honey if possible. I have tried this recipe a few times using cheaper brands of supermarket honey, and it doesn't whip up right.

Dragon's Beard Candy

YIELD: Makes 12 pieces

I've been eating dragon's beard candy for as long as I can remember. I loved watching the street vendors in Hong Kong pull and stretch a lump of sugar until it turned into 16,384 strands of silky white threads that got filled with finely chopped peanuts, sugar, and desiccated coconut before getting rolled into a delicate cocoon. It was reportedly invented by the chef to a Chinese emperor during the Han Dynasty, who after eating it got the strands stuck all over his face, resembling a dragon's beard. This is arguably the most difficult recipe in this book. It is a true art form and can take years to master. The sugar itself is not hard to make; it's the technique that needs practicing to pull into the most uniform silky, fine strands. That being said, I don't want to dissuade you from making it. It's delicious and tastes like a fluffy cloud of cereal. The wisps of sugar dissolve as they hit your tongue, leaving behind an array of crunchy, nutty textures. It's loads of fun and, even if it doesn't come out looking like the most perfect hair piece, it will still be totally worth it.

SUGAR BUNDLES

1 cup [200 g] granulated sugar
2½ Tbsp light corn syrup
½ tsp white vinegar
2 cups [280 g] cornstarch

FILLING

¼ cup [35 g] roasted almonds, finely chopped
¼ cup [10 g] freeze-dried bananas, finely chopped
½ cup [15 g] cornflakes, crushed

1 To make the sugar bundles, in a small pot, stir together the **sugar**, ⅓ cup [80 ml] of water, the **corn syrup**, and the **vinegar**. Bring to a boil over medium heat and continue to cook until it reaches 260°F [125°C].

2 While the syrup is heating, lightly grease a silicone donut mold with nonstick spray. You can use any heatproof, durable plastic cup or even a pint-size round deli container. Greasing is optional; I do it because it makes it way easier to pop out.

3 Once the syrup reaches 260°F [125°C], immediately remove the pot from the heat. Once the syrup stops bubbling, pour it into three cavities of the silicone donut mold and let cool to room temperature, 2 hours.

4 Meanwhile, prepare the filling. In a small bowl, stir together the **almonds, freeze-dried bananas,** and **cornflakes** until everything is evenly dispersed. Set aside until ready to use.

5 Place the **cornstarch** in a 9 by 13 in [23 by 33 cm] baking pan. Pop the sugar disc out of the mold and toss it in the cornstarch to coat. If you aren't using a donut mold, use a chopstick or skewer to poke a hole directly in the center of the disc and swirl it around until the opening is big enough to pull apart using your fingers.

6 Dunk the disc into the cornstarch again to coat. Place your fingers inside the center and gently start to stretch. Once the opening is big enough, start going around the circle like you are pulling a rope, trying to always maintain the same thickness and allowing the bottom of the loop to drag through the cornstarch.

7 Once you pull the loop to the length of the pan, twist and double the rope so you now have two loops. Dunk in the cornstarch to coat and repeat thirteen more times. As the strands get thinner, remember to generously coat them in the cornstarch so they don't stick together.

8 Break the rope off into twelve 8 in [20 cm] bundles. Place 1 to 2 tsp of the filling at one end of a bundle and roll it up to form a cocoon. Repeat with the rest and serve.

cont'd

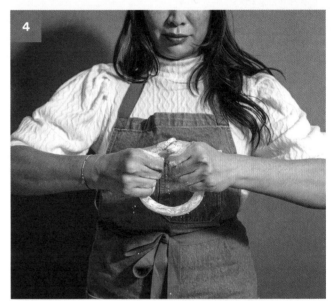

BREAKING BAO

28

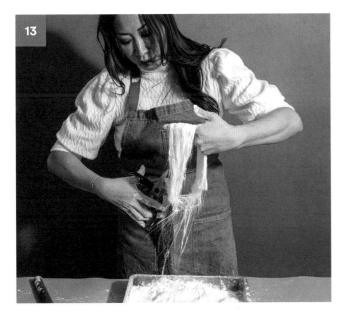

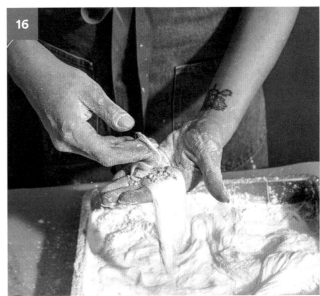

cont'd

BAO   CAKES & DESSERTS   SNACKS

Pro Tips & Storage

- Dragon's Beard candy is best eaten the day it's made.

- Please make sure your thermometer is calibrated properly before making this candy. You can check by boiling a pot of water; the thermometer should read 212°F [100°C]. If it doesn't, take note of how many degrees off it is and apply that difference when measuring the temperature of the sugar. Keep an eye on the temperature, and make sure to remove the syrup from the heat as soon as it reaches temp.

- The cornstarch keeps the strands from sticking back together, so make sure to constantly dust it.

- Humidity is a key factor in the success of this candy. I would not suggest trying to make it on a rainy day. The more humid it is, the higher the chance of the strands sticking back together.

- Really try to keep the width of the rope consistent all the way around.

- For a more traditional take, try filling it with a mixture of black sesame, coconut, and peanuts (see page 219).

White Rabbit Sachima

Sachima is a sweet snack originating from Manchuria made from deep-fried strips of fluffy dough held together with a sugar syrup, reminiscent of a Rice Krispies treat. The first time I had one was as a child. I recall seeing plates of them going past me on carts at dim sum and asking my parents what they were and could I have one? They are sweet and sticky, crunchy and chewy all at the same time. Every time we went to dim sum after that day, I kept my eyes peeled. Sadly, I haven't seen them offered in many other dim sum houses.

Because of their resemblance to Rice Krispies treats, I considered adding marshmallows here until I realized I could achieve the same look and better taste by using the confection that started it all: White Rabbit candies. If you read my introduction, you will know that this one candy is responsible for subconsciously setting me on a path to making the unrelatable relatable through food. There is so much that can be understood about one's culture through food, and limiting yourself to only exploring what is in your immediate circle can also limit possibilities. There are so many foods I am beyond happy to have been introduced to that make my life better, and I hope this is one of them for you.

YIELD: Makes one 8 in [20 cm] square pan

DOUGH

¾ cup + 1 Tbsp [120 g] all-purpose flour

1 large egg

1 large egg yolk

1 tsp granulated sugar

¼ tsp baking powder

¼ tsp baking soda

Pinch kosher salt

1 cup or 30 pieces [165 g] White Rabbit candy, unwrapped

4 cups [945 ml] vegetable oil

CARAMEL

½ cup + 1 Tbsp [115 g] granulated sugar

¼ cup [75 g] light corn syrup

1½ Tbsp honey

Pinch kosher salt

1 To make the dough, in the bowl of a stand mixer fitted with the dough hook attachment, combine the **flour, egg, egg yolk, sugar, baking powder, baking soda,** and **salt.** Knead on medium speed until smooth, 5 minutes. Transfer to a flour-dusted work surface and cover with a tea towel. Allow to rest for 30 minutes.

2 Meanwhile, place the **White Rabbit candy** in a food processor and process until the candies have broken up into tiny fragments the size of Nerds candy. Transfer to a bowl and set aside. If the humidity is high, it can cause the candy fragments to stick back together into one piece. In that case I recommend spreading it into one layer on a plate or baking sheet lined with parchment paper. Top with another piece of parchment and wrap in plastic wrap until ready to use.

3 In a wok or large heavy-bottomed pot over high heat, bring the **vegetable oil** to 350°F [180°C].

4 While the oil heats, line an 8 in [20 cm] square pan with parchment paper and grease the bottom and sides.

5 Dust your work surface with flour and roll the dough to a 12 by 16 in [30.5 by 40.5 cm] rectangle ¹⁄₁₆ inch [1.5 mm] thick. It should be as thin as a wonton wrapper. Cut in half lengthwise and place one layer on top of the other. Slice lengthwise into thirds then stack all the strips. Slice it once more in half lengthwise, and then cut ¼ in [6 mm] wide strips crosswise. Toss all the strips like noodles to loosen them and shake off any excess flour.

cont'd

6 Gently drop a handful of the strips into the oil. They will immediately puff up and float to the top. Continue to fry until golden brown, 1 to 2 minutes. Use a spider or slotted spoon to transfer them to a paper towel–lined baking sheet to drain. Repeat with the rest, frying in batches.

7 To make the caramel, in a large pot, stir together the **sugar**, **corn syrup**, 3 Tbsp of water, the **honey**, and the **salt**. Heat over medium-high until it reaches 250°F [120°C]. Remove from the heat.

8 Add the fried dough strips and stir to coat. Add the ground White Rabbit candy and mix until everything is evenly coated. Transfer to the prepared pan and press into an even layer. Allow to cool completely before cutting into squares.

Pro Tips & Storage

- The sachima can be stored in an airtight container for up to 3 days at room temperature.
- The dough can be made in advance and stored, double wrapped in plastic wrap, for up to 3 days in the refrigerator or 3 months in the freezer.
- The strips will puff up and expand a lot more than you would expect, so work in small batches.
- Try substituting marshmallows or cut-up pieces of mochi (see page 201) for the White Rabbit candy.

Acknowledgments

My parents were in their twenties when they met and had me. They were young immigrants in a new country trying to find their way to the American dream. Thinking back on what I was doing in my twenties, I can't possibly imagine trying to be that responsible or ambitious, let alone as a parent. I am sure they had other career ideas in mind for my sister and me, and the pressure was never easy. As the eldest child, I carried the weight of fulfilling the legacy of what they had worked so hard to provide; at times, many times, I crumbled under the burden. The path that they had perhaps hoped for was not the lane I would end up choosing. But little did they know, this path that I did choose, they are 100 percent responsible for. All the times my mom made my sister and me fresh pressed juice, a giant bowl of cut fruit, or pizza rolls resonated with me. All the snacks and delicacies they made us try from travels around the world would shape me. The numerous times my dad would trick me into eating something because it was good for my skin meant that he cared—at least enough to want me to be pimple-free. Telling my sister and me "You gotta eat" is equivalent to American families saying "I love you." So to Mommy and Daddy, this book is for you. Thank you for teaching me to love food, to travel, and to learn about other cultures. Thank you for always keeping me well fed. You gotta eat.

To Ilana Alperstein, thank you for believing in me, hearing my casual mention about wanting to write a book, and running with it.

To Kari Stuart, my amazing literary agent, thank you for showing me the ropes, teaching me the process, and making this happen. Thank you for your graceful patience and confidence in this project.

To Sarah Billingsley and the rest of the team at Chronicle Books, thank you for giving me this opportunity to share my story and for making my first book-writing experience relatively stress-free.

To my creative team, Evan Sung, Guillermo Riveros, and Audris Lam: Thank you to Evan, for being a genius and perfectly capturing my food. And to Guillermo and Audris for being as organized as possible and bringing my visions to life. Also to Audris, for being my prodigy little sister, for testing all the recipes, and for understanding and sharing so many experiences and food with me.

To my love Troy Hinson, thank you for always supporting me, believing in me, and talking me down from the ledge when I'm about to lose it. Thank you for exaggerating your face, noises, and enthusiasm every time you eat something I make.

To Christine Lau, the Clau to my Clam, thank you for bringing me on as pastry chef at you-know-where, which ultimately changed my course during la pandemia and got my wheels spinning over all the relative foods.

To all my friends who have supported me from day one, thank you. Especially to Tara and Ephy for testing, for sharing my love for production, and for your feedback and all your help.

One million thank-yous to you all. You have no idea how much I appreciate you and this experience. I never thought I would get this kind of opportunity to tell my story through food. I hope these recipes bring as much joy to you as they have to me.

Index

Chronicle Books publishes distinctive books and gifts. From award-winning children's titles, bestselling cookbooks, and eclectic pop culture to acclaimed works of art and design, stationery, and journals, we craft publishing that's instantly recognizable for its spirit and creativity. Enjoy our publishing and become part of our community at www.chroniclebooks.com.